MEETING OF MINDS

MEETING OF MINDS

The complete scripts, with illustrations, of the amazingly successful PBS-TV series.

THIRD SERIES

STEVE ALLEN

PROMETHEUS BOOKS • BUFFALO, NEW YORK

CONTENTS

INTRODUCTION

In the third year of production of "Meeting of Minds," one pair of programs represented something of a departure from the series' usual formula. The shows in question were subtitled "Shakespeare on Love." I had been intending, for some time, to invite William Shakespeare to be a guest, but in considering who the other members of his group might be, it suddenly occurred to me that, rather than confront him with illustrious figures from history, it might be interesting to introduce him to some of his own creatures.

Shakespeare, like most great literary artists, painted on a very wide canvas. Three of his characters—Hamlet, Romeo, and Othello—had difficulties with that emotion which, though the sweetest, has always been a source of suffering and misunderstanding for humankind, and what a damnably poignant reality that is. These famous three, I thought, would be wonderfully suitable choices. Certainly they had never before met their maker. It would be interesting to see what might happen if they were brought face to face.

In the original conception of "Meeting of Minds," the version I had tried to introduce on NBC television in 1958, the idea had been to limit each discussion to one general subject. There is nothing wrong with that formula, so far as it goes. There is certainly no doubt that stimulating discussions could be devised on democracy, war, pacifism, abortion, birth control, freedom, or any other significant idea. But it occurred to me, over the years during which I was occasionally attempting to make "Meeting of Minds" a television reality rather than merely a grand possibility, that we would learn relatively little about our famous guests themselves if we discussed only one broad subject with them.

There was also concern about the attention-span of even the more intelligent members of the American television audience. The decision gradually made itself, therefore, that while we would indeed have extended discussions on particularly important issues, we would, nevertheless, not limit our guests to a consideration of only one such issue. But now, as I began to develop the two programs featuring Shakespeare, I returned to the original formula and decided that it would be reasonable to deal with only the subject of love.

The title "Shakespeare on Love" flowed out at this point. And that was the name of the production that was eventually staged by the Shakespeare Society of America, at their theater in Los Angeles, that opened on May 26, 1975.

Although I served as host for the "Meeting of Minds" television series, I did not think it right to have a formal host or master-of-ceremonies for the theatrical production featuring Shakespeare. But there had to be someone who could provide more or less the same service, and yet be justified as part of the dramatic action. The solution: the Dark Lady of the Sonnets. Concerning this woman, very little indeed is known. For that matter, surprisingly little is known, with certainty, about Shakespeare himself, compared to what we know about, say, Martin Luther, Henry the VIII, or Abraham Lincoln.

It was obvious, once the theme of love had been selected, that we would have to deal with the famous sonnets. In reading them one day, it struck me that although Shakespeare and all his contemporaries had obviously spoken in the standard Elizabethan English common in his time, he was nevertheless perceived in such epic terms, because of his remarkable achievements, that it might be fun, and better art as well, to write the play, or at least the greater part of it, in Shakespearean-style iambic pentameter. While other writers might eventually have thought of this idea, only those who were themselves poets could have made it a reality, and, as it happens, I have written a good deal of verse since childhood, two volumes of which have been published.

Surrounding myself, then, during one three-day weekend, with collections of Shakespeare's plays and sonnets, I sat by the pool under a clear California blue sky and dictated the first draft of the play, needless to say quoting liberally from the three plays—*Hamlet, Romeo and Juliet,* and *Othello*—and the sonnets.

To enable the reader, before the curtain goes up so to speak, to judge how smoothly my own rhymed or rhythmic first lines harmonized with those of the master, I quote here a passage famous—among scholars at least—from *Othello,* concerning Jesus' advice that we love our enemies. The Moor says:

> That this is wisdom of a pure astounding beauty
> I'd be last to deny. But when we search
> for instances, examples, writs of proof,
> ah, there, 'twould seem, we enter realms so barren,
> were we to march abroad till we had found
> one single instance of a kiss bestowed
> on hated brow, one moment of sweet love
> for him who robs, or does us any harm,
> we'd march, I fear, to our unholy graves.

In case the reader is trying to recall in which specific scene of the play these lines are found, I confess to having played a trick. The lines are not of Shakespeare's creation, but are my own, written in imitation of his style. Our gifted actors made the seams connecting original to imitation quite invisible.

Even many otherwise well-informed people have always assumed, because of the soaring emotion of the sonnets, that since they were written by a man, they must have been written to, for, and about a woman. As it happens, however, for the most part this was not the case. How I dealt with this discovery provided a certain amount of the play's tension and humor.

When, some years later, I was doing the "Meeting of Minds" series for PBS, it was necessary to revise the script somewhat so as to place myself into it, since I was the host of the ongoing series. But I contrived to get myself offstage as quickly as possible and let the original players speak for themselves. The brilliant cast which made my fantasy believable consisted of my wife, Jayne Meadows, as the Dark Lady of the Sonnets, Desdemona, and Juliet; William Marshall as Othello; Anthony Costello as Hamlet; Charles Lanyer as Romeo; Harris Yulin as Shakespeare; and, in smaller roles, Fred Sadoff as Iago and the ghost of Hamlet's father.

*   *   *

Another pair of shows during our third year featured St. Augustine of Hippo of the fourth century, the first major Catholic philosopher, a man of remarkable intellect whose views are still influential; the flagrantly immoral Empress Theodora of the Byzantine Empire; Thomas Jefferson; and, one of our few guests from the twentieth century, Lord Bertrand Russell, one of the leading scholars of modern times.

Since the storyline of their discussion, so to speak, is made in the scripts of the two programs on which they appeared, there is little need to say more here. One factor, however, does require comment. In doing research on Jefferson, I drew part of my information from Fawn Brodie's insightful biography about him. Since Brodie is an authority on matters historical, while I certainly am not, I relied on her word as regards reports that Jefferson had a mistress who happened to be black. (To me this would be no more scandalous than if he had a mistress of his own color, but that is a point, of course, on which others will form their own opinions.) After the telecast of the two shows featuring Jefferson and the others, I heard from a number of historians who expressed strong reservations about the reliability of Brodie's reports concerning the story of Sally Hemmings. It is unlikely, I suppose, that the truth of the matter can ever be known, but I did want to state here that not all historians accept reports of a love relationship between Jefferson and Hemmings as reliable.

*   *   *

In that same season there was also a stimulating exchange involving Aristotle, Niccolo Machiavelli, Elizabeth Barrett Browning, and China's Sun Yat-Sen. I had, for some time, had a special interest in China and indeed not long after these programs would have the good fortune of being able to make three trips there, during one of which my son Bill and I were able to find his mother's birthplace. Jayne, as some readers may be aware, was born in China and spent the first seven years of her life there. She appeared on this pair of programs, too, as the delicate and romantic poet, and it was remarkable to see her move our studio audience to tears as she recited some of Browning's famous poems.

The most difficult portions of the scripts to write—of all four seasons—were those involving the philosophers. The reason, of course, is that they dealt chiefly with ideas. It is easy enough to relate stories about actions, confrontations, wars, atrocities, and scandals, but discussing abstract ideas was, as I say, somewhat difficult. Nevertheless, audiences reported no great difficulty in understanding what our visiting thinkers had to say.

SHOW # 13

St. Augustine of Hippo
(IVOR FRANCIS)

The Empress Theodora
of the Byzantine Empire
(SALOME JENS)

Thomas Jefferson
(SHEPPERD STRUDWICK)

Bertrand Russell
(JOHN HOYT)

Welcome to another Meeting of Minds.

Our guests this evening are St. Augustine of Hippo, of the fourth century.

The Empress Theodora of the Byzantine Empire of the sixth century.

From the eighteenth century . . . Thomas Jefferson.

And—from the twentieth century . . . Lord Bertrand Russell.

And now—your host—Mr. Steve Allen.

STEVE: Good evening, and welcome to another Meeting of Minds. Our first guest this evening—born in the year 354—is one of the most remarkable figures in the two-thousand-year history of Christianity. A genius, a philosopher, a creative theologian, and—in the view of the Catholic Church—a saint, which is to say an individual of heroic virtue.

But his influence extended beyond the bounds of Catholicism. He had an important effect on the Protestant leaders Martin Luther and John Calvin. . . .

RUSSELL: *(Offstage)* It wasn't my understanding, my dear fellow, that Augustine was to have the uninterrupted opportunity to—

AUGUSTINE: *(Offstage)* It is a matter of no great importance to me, your Lordship!

JEFFERSON: *(Offstage)* Gentlemen, I am sure each of us will have an opportunity to express his views. But we should let our host conduct the proceedings as he chooses.

STEVE: Wait a minute, there seems to be something—

(To camera) Loring, perhaps we should stop taping the—

JEFFERSON: *(He enters and approaches Steve.)* Mr. Allen.

STEVE: Ladies and gentlemen, our first guest to appear is not St. Augustine after all, but—as I am sure you recognize—the third president of the United States, Thomas Jefferson.

JEFFERSON: *(To audience)* Thank you. *(To Steve)* Mr. Allen, there seems to have been a misunderstanding. Lord Russell was under the impression that he was to participate in a debate. Consequently, when he heard you introducing Augustine, he objected to what he took to be the form of your program.

STEVE: Ah! Well, I had planned to interview Augustine for a few minutes before bringing in the. . . .

JEFFERSON: May I make a suggestion?

STEVE: Certainly.

JEFFERSON: If your plans are flexible it might be interesting at that to bring these two distinguished philosophers out together since they seem to have already begun their argument in the waiting room.

STEVE: Mr. President, you have a good sense of theater. That's a capital suggestion. Since I've already introduced Augustine, I'll say a few words about Mr. Russell, by way of introduction.

Could I trouble you to find out if both gentlemen are prepared to enter on those terms?

JEFFERSON: It would be my pleasure. Oh, gentlemen—*(He exits.)*

STEVE: Oh, and you might let me know of Her Majesty's wishes in all this. Or is she upstairs?

(To camera.) Pardon me, ladies and gentlemen. I hope there will be no further delay.

Having Bertrand Russell appear with us represents something of a departure in that he does not come to us out of one earlier century or another but died only a few years ago.

It's sometimes risky to hazard a guess as to which of one's contemporaries will be remembered a hundred, or a thousand, years into the future. But there can be little doubt about Bertrand Russell's importance.

His contributions to philosophy and mathematics are significant, and he's one of those philosophers who do not simply observe events from relative isolation, but rather play an active part in the social drama of their times.

As with all men of great knowledge and vision, his views were ahead of their time and caused him to be despised in certain quarters. In 1903 he was branded a "devil's minister" because he said a free man should worship as he saw fit and not as instructed by the churches. In 1940 he was refused a post at the City College of New York because of his views on sex and marriage; and in 1961 he was jailed in England because he took part in demonstrations against nuclear warfare. So—

Ladies and gentlemen . . . Bertrand Russell. *(Russell enters, bows, and hurries to the table.)* *(Superimpose: Bertrand Russell 1872–1970)*

STEVE: Good evening, sir. Er—where is Augustine?

RUSSELL: He's having a word with Mr. Jefferson. He seems quite upset.

STEVE: Oh, dear. I hope he won't disappoint us. Well . . . I imagine it must be very exciting for you to meet St. Augustine of Hippo.

RUSSELL: Indeed, sir. He was one of the most remarkable figures of Western history. A passionate man, in youth certainly very far from a model of virtue, but driven by an inner impulse to search for truth and righteousness. May I sit?

STEVE: Oh, certainly. Forgive me.

RUSSELL: Like Tolstoy, Augustine was obsessed—in his later years—
by a sense of sin, which made his life stern and his philosophy—
in my view—inhuman. He actually said, "Cursed is everyone who
places his hope in man."

Augustine assailed heresies vigorously, as you probably know,
but it's interesting that some of his own views—when repeated by
Jansenius in the seventeenth century—were pronounced heretical
by the Catholic Church. *(With a smile)* Although the Church had
never impugned their orthodoxy until the Protestants took up his
opinions and championed them. Where is the fellow?

STEVE: I'll go look, in a moment.

RUSSELL: Very well. Perhaps he feels guilty at having gotten angry
at me!

STEVE: Guilty?

RUSSELL: Yes. You see, one of the first experiences related in his famous *Confessions* occurred in his boyhood and shows—really—
that he was a very normal young fellow.

It appears that with some companions of his own age he raided
a neighbor's pear tree, although he was not hungry, and his parents
had better pears at home. Augustine continued throughout his life
to consider this an act of almost incredible wickedness.

STEVE: Is that right?

RUSSELL: In any event, I am, as you say, extremely gratified to meet
him.

But you see, with all due respect Mr. Allen, I would question
whether you are—well, I shan't say intelligent enough—but informed enough to counter the arguments of our distinguished theologian.

STEVE: Well, even if I were, your Lordship, I wouldn't dream of debat-
ing a single point with one of the most powerful thinkers the world
has ever known.

RUSSELL: *(With a smile)* Why ever not? But, in any event, I wish merely
to establish that many of the learned doctor's observations which
are not irrefutable ought to be appropriately refuted.

STEVE: As you wish. Ladies and gentlemen, it is an honor indeed to
present Aurelius Augustinus, Bishop of the town of Hippo. *(Augustine enters.)* *(Superimpose: St. Augustine, A.D. 354-430)* I introduced you as Aurelius Augustinus of *Hippo,* Father. That might
be unclear to some in our audience.

AUGUSTINE: Hippo was a city in Africa. It was there that I was elected a bishop of the Christian church, and it was there I spent the last half of my life. It was chiefly in Hippo that I formed my philosophical concepts.

STEVE: In what part of the African continent was the—

AUGUSTINE: North Africa, in what is now known as Algeria. My parents lived in Tágaste.

STEVE: Your people were—

AUGUSTINE: They were Berbers.

STEVE: Your mind works so quickly I don't even have to finish my sentences.

AUGUSTINE: The word comes from the Roman *barbari,* which is related to your word *barbarian.*

STEVE: It's difficult to think of you, Father, as in any way related to the word *barbarian.*

AUGUSTINE: *(chuckles)* But, perhaps I should point out that I didn't begin my life as a Christian. My mother, Monica, was a Christian but she was very much in the minority in our community.

STEVE: What language did you speak?

AUGUSTINE: Numidian. My country was called Numidia. But those of us who were fairly well-educated spoke Latin as well.

STEVE: Your mother had great influence over you, I understand. Incidentally, there's a community not far from where we sit named after her, Santa Monica.

AUGUSTINE: Is that right? Well, my mother was a totally dedicated woman. She believed in Christ and never wavered in her belief.

I finally realized how right she was, and how just and wise the teachings of Christ were. But I was thirty-two years old when I was baptized. As a young fellow I had been a hedonist.

STEVE: Hedonist. One who lives for pleasure.

AUGUSTINE: *(To audience.)* Like many of you moderns.

RUSSELL: Ah. I suppose we are to assume that pleasure is evil, as you did, Augustine. You, who were so troubled by the perfectly natural function of sex. You who said to God, please give me chastity, but not yet.

Who was it, Augustine, that gave us the capacity for feeling the pleasures of the senses?

AUGUSTINE: It was God, who gave us all things.

RUSSELL: Then why are you so fearful of this marvelous example of his handiwork?

AUGUSTINE: We may make either a moral or an im-moral use of the sensory pleasures. *(He glowers.)*

But I shall deal with you later, Russell!

RUSSELL: I await your pleasure. If I may use the word.

AUGUSTINE: Anyway, Mr. Allen, I drank heavily, I caroused, I indulged in the bodily pleasures. I tell you this to correct any impression you may have about my coming into life as a naturally saintly fellow. Oh, no; it took years for me to see the error of my ways.

STEVE: Could you be more specific?

AUGUSTINE: I'll spare you the full details of a misspent youth. My parents were of modest means but they managed to gather together enough money to give me a good education.

I was sent to Carthage, the great town of our province, where I studied languages and oratory, with the idea of becoming a civil servant.

STEVE: Were you a good student?

AUGUSTINE: Yes, but a spiritual drifter. In those days I had a great deal of what you might call fun. But with time I realized there was no true satisfaction in this "fun." I, quite literally, hungered for something in which to believe and, possibly as a rebellion against parental authority, was willing to try almost every religion but Christianity.

But eventually, through my mother's persistence, I came around to a confidence in Christ.

My studies had taken me to Rome and later Milan. It was there I was converted, partly through the efforts of that wonderful man you know as St. Ambrose.

Two years later, I returned to North Africa, with the object of retiring to meditation. I established a monastic community in which there was no right to private property.

STEVE: No private property?

AUGUSTINE: No, our brothers held everything in common. But, the church considered my abilities might better be used in administration and teaching. I was elected Bishop of Hippo and gradually became more and more involved in writing and spreading the Gospel of Jesus.

STEVE: Christians today generally assume, Father, when they look at the sad spectacle of thousands of different Christian churches and sects, that in the early days of Christian history unity was the norm.

RUSSELL: Do they really? Unfortunately unity has rarely been the norm, in any important area of human activity.

AUGUSTINE: Quite so, your Lordship. There was, of course, in my time something identifiable as the Christian church, but we were very troubled by doctrinal disputes and factional divisions.

RUSSELL: Yes, these arguments among the followers of Jesus started at least as early as the time of St. Paul.

AUGUSTINE: I referred not merely to arguments, sir, but to fundamental doctrinal divisions. There were, for example, the Donatists, the Pelagians, the Arians—

STEVE: Who were the Donatists?

AUGUSTINE: You might describe them as a sort of right wing of the church. They were—to use your modern expression—more Catholic than the Pope.

You see, the pagan Roman Emperor Diocletian, early in the fourth century—had severely persecuted Christians. In this time of terror a certain number of priests—understandably enough—did not find within themselves the strength to become martyrs. The Donatist Christians were infuriated by such weakness and considered such priests traitors to Christ.

STEVE: Really?

RUSSELL: Yes. This led to a full century of violence in which the Donatists became the most powerful Christian faction in Africa.

Would you agree, Father, that the Donatists were religious fanatics?

AUGUSTINE: Indeed I would. Like all such fanatics the Donatists imagined that they were gifted at separating the good from the wicked or weak.

STEVE: You mentioned the Pelagians. Who were they?

AUGUSTINE: Well, the Donatists—who were named after Bishop Donatus of Carthage—were active in North Africa. The Pelagians came out of the West. Pelagius himself was a monk of the British Isles who visited Rome—near the close of the fourth century— and while there wrote a commentary on the Epistles of St. Paul.

He was personally a good man, in many ways, but very mistaken in his opinions on Original Sin.

STEVE: Perhaps since the theory of Original Sin is—

AUGUSTINE: *(Correcting him)* The doctrine of Original Sin.

STEVE: Perhaps since the idea of Original Sin has been so remarkably influential for so many centuries, we should briefly clarify it here.

AUGUSTINE: It means, very simply, that when God created man, He created him innocent, pure, and holy, but that man chose to become sinfully disobedient. And that—

RUSSELL: Man, you say? The whole human race made such a decision?

AUGUSTINE: No. Man in the person of Adam.

RUSSELL: Then you believe that if Jones, let us say, performs an evil act, Smith somehow shares the blame for that sin, in the total absence of any actual personal involvement!

AUGUSTINE: No, Mr. Russell. I believe, however, that both Smith and Jones are sinful because of—as a direct result of—the sin of Adam.

RUSSELL: I intended Jones to represent Adam.

STEVE: Gentlemen, forgive me, but I've just realized that we've left President Jefferson waiting in the hall!

RUSSELL: Oh, dear. Bring him into our conversation with the learned doctor, by all means. Like Thomas Paine and Benjamin Franklin, and many other American thinkers of your revolutionary times, Jefferson was a good Deist, and quite knowledgeable about religious questions.

And no doubt Her Christian Majesty, the Empress Theodora, would care to join us.

STEVE: I very much hope so. Well, first, our third president, chief author of the American Declaration of Independence, one of the Founding Fathers—again—Thomas Jefferson. *(Jefferson enters.)* *(Superimpose: Thomas Jefferson 1743-1826)* Welcome, Mr. President. Would you care to take part in our theological discussion?

JEFFERSON: Well, I certainly don't want to speak at great length on the subject of religion. At least I never did so in my lifetime. My beliefs are simple. I believe that the ethical teachings of Christ are benevolent and sublime. The terrible irony is that those teachings have caused some of His followers to become intolerant of others who interpret them differently. Consequently for long centuries we have had people slaughtering each other in the name of Christianity.

AUGUSTINE: But, Mr. President, you must not assume that such actions are the fault of Christianity.

RUSSELL: You say it is not the fault of Christians if they commit such hideous crimes?

AUGUSTINE: It happens, sir, because man relies on his baser instincts in trying to persuade others. The only true persuasion is by love.

JEFFERSON: Then, Father, perhaps the churches should not be so dogmatic.

AUGUSTINE: And why not? The truth must be asserted and defended! And vigorously!

RUSSELL: *(Smiling)* Ahhh! "The Truth."

JEFFERSON: *(He chuckles.)* I recall a sermon by a very persuasive Quaker minister who told his congregation that in heaven God knew no distinction, but considered all good men as his children and as brethren of the same family.

I believe, as did that Quaker minister, that he who steadily observes those moral precepts in which almost all religions concur will never be questioned at the gates of heaven as to the dogmas in which they differ!

AUGUSTINE: I wish I could agree, sir, but—you see—points of dogma do have their profound importance.

RUSSELL: Well, we had just gotten to the dogma of Original Sin. Augustine here thought most of mankind would roast in the actual flames of hell—for all eternity—because of that damnable belief.

AUGUSTINE: *(Putting him on.)* "Damnable"?

JEFFERSON: Well, since the debate on the question remains unsettled I would observe only that the great majority of the human race no longer agrees with you on that point, Father.

AUGUSTINE: Truth, Mr. President, is not arrived at by democratic processes.

JEFFERSON: Nor by sectarian speculation.

AUGUSTINE: *(With a smile)* In any event, Pelagius, unfortunately, would agree with his British countryman Lord Russell that humans were *not* tainted by Adam's fall, and are therefore not absolutely compelled to sin.

Pelagius felt that it was within the capacity of humans to act virtuously and that they did not therefore require any special, direct help from God to do so.

RUSSELL: Quite. Most thoughtful people of the modern age would find Pelagius a rather attractive figure. He preached reason, moderation, and personal responsibility.

In other words, he said that if you commit a sin, it is your fault, not Adam's.

AUGUSTINE: *(With a smile)* I understand that the Freudians have somewhat undermined the Pelagian position in the modern world, your Lordship.

RUSSELL: *(He laughs, acknowledging Augustine's cleverness.)* Yes! But not nearly as much as Dr. Freud undermined your position, Father.

STEVE: Thank you, gentlemen. But we're getting ahead of your personal story, Father. Let's return to your early days, if we may.

AUGUSTINE: Yes. After the death of my father, a wealthy friend—a man named Romanianus—was kind enough to pay my way to the city of Carthage where—as I mentioned—I took up the study of rhetoric—the art of eloquence.

In the year 374—I was then nineteen years old—I returned from

Carthage and began teaching grammar. I had to earn a living, you see, not only to support my two-year-old son but also—

STEVE: Oh, you had gotten married in Carthage?

AUGUSTINE: No. I had taken a mistress, not a wife.

STEVE: What was the woman's name?

AUGUSTINE: In my *Confessions* I give full details of my early life, hiding nothing, revealing my sins. But I refused to give the name of the woman I loved.

RUSSELL: Do you think, Mr. Allen, that since we've come to the charming subject of romantic love, we ought to ask Her Majesty to join us? No doubt *her* thoughts on the subject would be instructive.

JEFFERSON: Marvelous idea.

STEVE: Very well.

JEFFERSON: You know, gentlemen, whatever we might say—in praise or blame—about the world in which the Roman Emperor Justinian and his Empress Theodora lived, we would be well advised to keep in mind that theirs was a thoroughly Christian society.

AUGUSTINE: *(Somewhat annoyed)* I wouldn't say "thoroughly."

STEVE: Well, we have, on Meeting of Minds, presented philosophers, scientists, political leaders, artists, writers, military men. Obviously, this is hardly the kind of forum to which we would invite strip-tease dancers, entertainers, clowns, or prostitutes. Yet—incredibly enough—we are at the moment welcoming a woman who—in her youth—was all of those things.

But, like Augustine, she renounced her sinful ways and—

AUGUSTINE: I resent the comparison, sir!

STEVE: I intended no offense, Father.

Well, here is a truly remarkable personage, who transcended her scandalous beginnings and became the most powerful woman in the world in her day—which was the sixth century—the Empress Theodora! *(As she enters, all stand.) (Superimpose: The Empress Theodora 508–548)* Welcome, Your Majesty.

THEODORA: Gentlemen.

STEVE: Your Majesty, the Byzantine Empire, which you and your husband ruled, was such a—

THEODORA: Just a moment, sir. As for my "scandalous beginnings," I did not choose the circumstances of my early life!

My critics were scandalized because I broke through the boundaries of caste that protected the privileges of the aristocracy. Roman law in my day specified that no citizen could marry an actress!

I changed all that!

RUSSELL: Yes, you see, Mr. Allen, prostitution itself in that day was an accepted part of life in a Christian empire.

STEVE: I see. Well, just how did you go about changing the law?

THEODORA: Justinian, who was a senator—most likely successor to the throne—was in love with me. He appealed to his uncle the Emperor Justinian, and the law was changed.

STEVE: Your Majesty, since you were not born to royalty, or even the aristocracy—er—forgive me for perhaps seeming indelicate—

THEODORA: Or rude. No, sir. I progressed from the gutter—is that what you want to know?—from the gutter to the highest seats of power, and in a short period of time.

JEFFERSON: In Her Majesty's defense, gentlemen, we must recognize the sort of—er, background from which she emerged.

STEVE: Yes. That is, if one can believe what the historian Procopius said about her.

THEODORA: Sir, I'm sure all of us will be pleased if our presence here leads any of the millions listening to refer to published work written about us. Or by us. But I would say a cautionary word against referring to only *one* source.

(*To Steve*) Forgive me for not being informed about your own exploits, if any, but may I correctly assume you have done nothing to merit mention in the annals of history?

STEVE: You are all too correct, Your Majesty.

THEODORA: I assumed as much. But since you are evidently a public figure I assume that the journalists and biographers of the present day do, from time to time, make mention of you.

STEVE: They do indeed.

THEODORA: And do you find all the published reports of your doings accurate, in every detail?

STEVE: No. As a matter of fact, journalists have now been writing about me for over thirty years, and in all that time there have been very few stories that did not have *some* errors in them.

THEODORA: Bear that in mind when you are consulting the works of historians who wrote about the truly important personages of history. Never mind the insults of Procopius.

STEVE: Yes, I've often wondered why Procopius was so severe in his criticism of you.

THEODORA: Procopius—who worked in our court—was impressed with the aristocrats of Constantinople. I was not an aristocrat. Procopius was one of many who resented the fact that I had started life in the Hippodrome.

STEVE: The Hippodrome?

THEODORA: Yes, the circus in Constantinople. The scene of games, races, public meetings, bawdy shows.

He was envious that, I, having come from a level of society lower than slavery, rose to become an Empress!

He didn't have the guts to write about me when I was alive!

JEFFERSON: For a very good reason, I would think.

STEVE: Which was?

THEODORA: I would have had him killed.

He depicted me as a backstairs politician. He claimed my husband, Justinian, was under my thumb and said that I influenced his decisions of state!

STEVE: Did you?

THEODORA: Certainly! Justinian sought my advice.

STEVE: But how could you consider yourself qualified to help rule the enormous empire that—

THEODORA: *(Interrupting)* First of all, do you moderns even know what the Byzantine Empire was? Do you know how it came to exist?

STEVE: Any assumptions you might make about our ignorance of history, Your Majesty, are probably all too well founded.

THEODORA: Very well. Let us go back—even before St. Augustine's time—to the third century, when the Roman Empire had reached its greatest geographical limits. It included not only Italy and the areas I assume you do know about—Asia Minor, Egypt, Syria, the Mediterranean areas of North Africa—but also Balkan territories in Eastern Europe, as well as Spain, France, and England.

STEVE: Incredible.

RUSSELL: Yes. Particularly when we recall that such an enormous empire was maintained in a day when there were no telephones, no radio, no airplanes, no modern communications or transportation of any kind.

THEODORA: We did have a system of conveying simple messages—from hilltops—by reflected sunlight.

But the Empire was beginning to decay.

STEVE: In what ways, specifically?

RUSSELL: Monetary inflation was rampant. The governing classes were corrupt.

AUGUSTINE: They were also guilty of sexual excesses, interested in luxury, in their own gratification.

THEODORA: *(She gives him a sharp look.)* Yes, like you in your youth, Augustine.

AUGUSTINE: And you in yours, Your Majesty.

RUSSELL: The Emperors also had trouble with barbarian invaders.

THEODORA: Yes. In time it became clear that much of the wealth of the Empire, its basic necessities, came from the eastern areas.

In A.D. 286 the Emperor Diocletian, a great reformer, had decided to divide the Roman Empire into two separate geographical sections.

STEVE: Why?

THEODORA: To make it easier to administer.

AUGUSTINE: By the fourth century, however, Constantine had done away with Diocletian's two-province system and had reestablished the Emperor's control over both the western and eastern territories.

THEODORA: That is correct, Father, but Constantine realized that the eastern half of the Roman Empire was now truly the more important. Consequently he left both Rome and the city of Milan behind and selected a new site for his capitol, the ancient Greek settlement of Byzantium.

Here he had a new city constructed, which he named after himself, Constantinople. The formal dedication ceremonies took place in the year 330.

AUGUSTINE: Constantine will, of course, be remembered for something far more important than having founded a city. After being converted to Christianity himself he decided that Christianity would now be the officially favored religion of the Roman Empire.

JEFFERSON: Thus setting a most unfortunate precedent of the union of Christian church and state!

STEVE: Mr. President, it's something of a cliché of political rhetoric among Americans to be very critical of the union of church and state. If I may play devil's advocate for a moment, exactly what is so bad about cooperation between church and state?

JEFFERSON: In theory, perhaps nothing at all, Mr. Allen. But in reality the union of church and state has never failed to bring about the most destructive consequences.

AUGUSTINE: Surely, Mr. President, you would not want to suggest that its results have been totally evil.

JEFFERSON: Oh, of course not. It may, obviously, be productive of some good, if the powers of the state are directed toward the encouragement of morality, let us say. And if we are discussing a hypothetical situation in which all the inhabitants of a given nation are affiliated with one particular religion, then there might be something, at least . . . well, efficient about such an arrangement. But in the world of reality we observe that there are no such instances. There is always a dissident minority.

Consequently in those nations where the church has been able to call upon the secular arm we have witnessed the most horrible and certainly un-Christian persecutions, slaughters, pogroms. There is never the slightest excuse for such tyranny!

Christians did not like it very much when they were persecuted by Roman Emperors loyal to the old pagan religions! Therefore Christians have no right to persecute others when they are in the majority.

Would you agree, Your Majesty?

THEODORA: Absolutely not! Augustine is right about this!

RUSSELL: Hmmm. Strange bedfellows. *(To Augustine)* No offense intended, Bishop.

STEVE: Well, I'm sorry, Your Majesty. You were telling us about the Byzantine Empire—

THEODORA: Yes. Well, during the fourth and fifth centuries—as I've said—the Roman Empire began to crumble. The Goths, the Ostrogoths, and the Visigoths took control of large areas. The Vandals seized the North African Roman provinces.

It's at this point in history that my husband Justinian appears on the scene.

STEVE: I'm curious to know what sort of man Justinian was.

THEODORA: A sincere, dedicated Christian, loyal to your church, Augustine.

By the way, did I hear you say you truly loved your mistress?

AUGUSTINE: Yes.

THEODORA: Then it was a relationship of more than passion?

AUGUSTINE: Yes, Your Majesty.

THEODORA: So was my relationship with Justinian.

But we married, Father. You did not. Why?

AUGUSTINE: The human heart is restless, Your Majesty, and knows no peace until it rests in God. Marriage was not for me. I gave up my mistress.

STEVE: But by that time you had not been reached by the message of Christ, Father. What figures before your time had made an impression on you?

AUGUSTINE: I had a great admiration for Cicero. I also admired Plato.

RUSSELL: And were greatly influenced by him.

AUGUSTINE: Indeed. And after returning home to Tágaste I read—with great excitement—Aristotle's *Categories*. I was at the time—by religion—a Manichaean. But my readings began to weaken my faith.

STEVE: Could you enlighten us about the religion of Manichaeism?

AUGUSTINE: Certainly. The faith was named after a Babylonian prophet of the third century named Mani. He angered the Persian authorities of the time—

RUSSELL: And their priests—

AUGUSTINE: Yes. As a result he was either crucified or skinned alive; the record is not clear.

RUSSELL: I suppose the distinction cannot have mattered very much to poor Mani.

AUGUSTINE: In any event Mani saw the world as a struggle between the kingdom of light—ruled by the Father of Greatness—and the kingdom of darkness—ruled by the Devil.

RUSSELL: It would be misleading, Father, to suggest that Manichaeism had no connection whatever with Christianity.

AUGUSTINE: You're quite right, Lord Russell. We Manichaeans respected Jesus as the guide of the souls.

RUSSELL: Yes, the sect was quite similar to Christianity in a number of particulars.

STEVE: Oh, how do you mean?

RUSSELL: The Manichaeans believed in prayer and fasting, baptism, a sort of Lord's Supper. They had an annual feast to celebrate Mani's execution and ascension into heaven.

STEVE: Father, how did your beliefs as a Manichaean influence the way you lived?

AUGUSTINE: We ate no meat, drank no wine, and did not use impure language. Also we Manichaeans took vows to do no menial labor.

THEODORA: An easy enough decision in a time when servants and slaves were readily available.

AUGUSTINE: Lastly, we did not marry.

STEVE: No wonder there are none of you left.

RUSSELL: More importantly, the Manichaeans also were of the opinion that one could reason one's way to a belief in God and religious truth generally.

AUGUSTINE: Yes. This was what initially attracted me to the Manichaean faith.

RUSSELL: What is absolutely fascinating here is that many years later—after Augustine had been converted to orthodox Christianity—and had begun to develop his own theories, his absolutely central idea—which a thousand years later affected Luther, Calvin, and countless other Protestants and Catholics—was that belief must come before understanding.

AUGUSTINE: Yes, I concede that pure unaided reason cannot lead men to certain knowledge of the existence of God, and all that follows from such a belief, but that one must simply believe first and that understanding could then follow.

JEFFERSON: You know, Mr. Allen, Augustine's account of the precise moment of his conversion is singularly dramatic, in case you're not familiar with its details.

STEVE: No, I'm not, but I have long been fascinated by the process of conversion itself. It would be a relatively simple phenomenon to consider if everyone in the world who was converted traveled in the same direction. But apparently every day now people are converted to one religion or another. Others are suddenly converted to a political philosophy.

But, I have the impression that one factor common to practically all sudden conversions is that they take place in the context of severe emotional distress. Was that true in your own case, Father?

AUGUSTINE: Yes. I had long been troubled by a sense of my own sinfulness.

STEVE: Precisely what was it that was troubling you?

AUGUSTINE: The very toy of toys, and vanities of vanities: My ancient mistresses still held me. They seemed to be whispering to me, "Why hast thou cast us off?" I missed them, I longed for them, yet what defilements did they suggest, what shame? I wished to move forward through life—alone, self-sufficient—but I could not resist looking back at them.

But suddenly, as I stood in a quiet garden, I seemed to see another figure, the chaste dignity of Continency, serene, with hands stretching forth to embrace me, her holy hands full of multitudes of good examples. For I knew that there were so many young men and maidens—people of all ages—who had willingly, and successfully, sacrificed the pleasures of the flesh. And the spirit of this virtue seemed to smile at me as with a sweet mockery, as if to say, "Can *you* not do what these youths—what these maidens—can do, with the help of the Lord their God?"

My close friend Alypius sat beside me, in silence, perhaps reading my thoughts. Suddenly within me there arose a mighty storm, bringing a full shower of tears.

I turned away from Alypius, in some embarrassment, seeking solitude.

I cast myself down under a nearby fig tree, weeping as I'd never wept before.

I spoke to my God, saying, "How long, how long? Why not now? Why not is there at this very hour an end to my uncleanness?"

Suddenly I heard, from a neighboring house, a child's voice chanting the phrase, "Take up and read. Take up and read." It seemed strange to me that so young a child would say anything of the sort. I arose at once, interpreting the message to be no other than a command from God to open a book and read the first chapter I might find.

I hurried back to where Alypius was sitting and opened the pages of the New Testament! I read, "Not in rioting and drunkenness, not in chambering and wantonness, not in strife and envying. But put ye on the Lord Jesus Christ, and make no provision for the flesh in concupiscence."

STEVE: Well, thank you, Father. . . .

But, Your Majesty, we need to know still more about your background in order to understand your later views, and actions. What did your father do?

THEODORA: My poor father worked in the Hippodrome.

STEVE: What was the Hippodrome like?

THEODORA: It was an incredible place. Backstage there were wild animals, racehorses, chariot drivers, athletes, actors, actresses, acrobats, jugglers, prostitutes, dancers, gamblers, whore-masters.

JEFFERSON: Yes. It was a center not only for sports and theatrical entertainment, but vice, corruption, political activity.

STEVE: What did your father do there?

THEODORA: He was an animal trainer. It cost him his life.

STEVE: How?

THEODORA: He was killed by one of his bears, which left my mother and my two sisters and me destitute. All we could do to avoid starvation was perform the most menial of circus jobs.

JEFFERSON: I understand that people had sometimes been slaughtered in the Hippodrome.

THEODORA: Yes, criminals were sometimes killed there. You kill your criminals today, don't you?

STEVE: Yes. We are starting to again.

THEODORA: Lions and leopards would attack each other. Gladiators would fight beasts before screaming crowds!

AUGUSTINE: So many dreadful things took place in the Hippodrome, Mr. Jefferson, that I suspect had you been able to look in on it your faith in the wisdom of the masses might have been considerably weakened.

JEFFERSON: It comes as no news to me, Father, that mobs are capable of savagery and madness. But the people do have a certain wisdom if they are properly informed, properly educated!

THEODORA: Well, from such a hell-hole it was an advancement to serve in a brothel, believe me!

JEFFERSON: As a young woman?

THEODORA: No. As a child! I was only ten when I became an assistant, along with my sisters. Only a few years later I was required to perform the full functions of a prostitute.

Yes, gentlemen, a prostitute by the time I was thirteen. And not by choice, Father! But as the price of poverty!

STEVE: I understand that you shortly elevated yourself from the status of prostitute to that of actress.

THEODORA: I became an actress, sir, but there was no elevation. As I've explained, Roman law forbade marriage of a citizen to any woman who had appeared on the stage.

RUSSELL: Yes, our friend, Augustine, felt great guilt about the fact that in his early days he had enjoyed the theater.

THEODORA: Well, the idea that an actress might also be respectable or virtuous is very modern, I assure you. We had no higher social standing than did racehorses. For long centuries the church would not permit actors or actresses to be buried on consecrated ground. Today the church permits your Mafia murderers to be buried in such soil!

But do you know why I succeeded, despite my background, when thousands of others of my kind did not?

STEVE: Because of your beauty?

THEODORA: Nonsense. There were other whores as attractive as I was, some no doubt even more so. But, the fact is that I was a popular entertainer; I'm not ashamed to say it.

The art of comedy was appreciated in my day, as it is in yours, and I had natural gifts for it. I would do anything to make audiences laugh—lift my skirts, cross my eyes. *(She does so.)*

STEVE: Comedy, Your Majesty, has not improved all that much in the past fourteen centuries. (*Theodora smiles.*)

RUSSELL: Were you not also famed for your wit, Your Majesty?

THEODORA: As much as you were for yours, Lord Russell. And wherever you find wit, you find intelligence.

Although Justinian was a man of the world when I met him, he remained faithful to me—absolutely faithful.

Had he been interested only in physical beauty, no doubt he could have done better. But it was my mind that held him.

JEFFERSON: And your courage, no doubt.

THEODORA: Yes, Mr. President! For I'd seen the worst side of human behavior. I'd known hunger, vile poverty, danger, and had survived them all.

So I did *far* more than provide Justinian with just the physical pleasures *(to Augustine),* which as a good Christian husband he had every right to expect.

STEVE: Your Majesty, you haven't quite made clear. . . . How did you progress from being a courtesan to a woman of such high rank?

THEODORA: Ah, what a lovely word, courtesan. The only difference between a whore and a courtesan is the amount of money the man has to spend.

STEVE: But how did you become so—er—successful?

THEODORA: You are naive, sir. A courtesan becomes successful for two reasons. First, she is good at her job. But even more importantly she has the good fortune to meet the right people.

STEVE: And who did you meet?

THEODORA: A Tyrian nobleman named Hekebolus. He had just been appointed governor of the African city that you now call Bengasi, in the modern nation of Libya.

To celebrate his appointment he held a party for his friends; I was invited. Hekebolus was attracted to me and asked me to accompany him to Africa. I asked if I could be his wife. He said no; it was against the law. So I went as his mistress.

Well, in time I became bored with Hekebolus. Life in his mansion was dull, and he paid me so little attention I might as well have been his wife. The governor and I had a misunderstanding.

STEVE: What did you do then?

THEODORA: I made my way to Alexandria.

STEVE: How old were you at the time?

THEODORA: Barely eighteen. To this point my life had had very little direction. I was ill, in dire poverty. I took to a convent, where I recuperated, but soon realized that I was unsuited for convent life.

AUGUSTINE: I should think so.

THEODORA: I did, however, become a sincere Christian in Alexandria,

Father! Later I returned to Constantinople, determined to put my sinful life behind me. Unfortunately my poor sisters were still working there, as prostitutes.

Eventually, through a woman I had known during my days as an entertainer, I met Justinian. It was not long after our first meeting that he said he was in love with me.

STEVE: Your Majesty, did you feel in any way—er—socially inferior to Justinian when you first met him?

THEODORA: Why should I? He was the son of a peasant! However, he had received a superlative education, and I saw the potential for greatness in him.

STEVE: Your Majesty, on our screen at the moment we are showing a mosaic of your husband, made during his lifetime. Is it a good likeness?

THEODORA: Not particularly. It was originally a representation of Theodoric, king of the Goths. After the Roman reconquest, the small tiles were altered to make the features resemble those of Justinian.

It was in the year 525 that we were married, in the magnificent church of Santa Sophia that Emperor Constantine had built two centuries earlier. Two years later, after the old emperor Justin died, the patriarch of Constantinople crowned Justinian Emperor and myself Empress!

JEFFERSON: Imagine the drama of the triumphal procession, gentlemen, in which dignitaries of state and church, soldiers and courtiers, all marched to the Hippodrome so Her Majesty and Justinian could receive the acclamations of their adoring subjects.

THEODORA: Imagine it indeed, gentlemen! The Hippodrome—once the scene of my degradation, now the theater of my greatest triumph!

STEVE: Did you have any difficulty, Your Majesty, in your new role as Empress?

THEODORA: None whatever. As Empress, I gave my greatest performance.

STEVE: What was your attitude toward prostitution after you had reformed your own habits, Your Majesty, and married Justinian?

THEODORA: I could no more abolish it than you can today. But I did close up those brothels where the girls were shamelessly exploited! I lectured the managers severely, gave them payment in gold for their girls, told them to close up their houses and seek other occupations. I then sent for the girls, gave them money and new clothes, and sent them home to their parents or to a convent of repentance, which I opened for the homeless.

STEVE: What about those who wished to remain in the trade?

THEODORA: For them I outlawed homosexuality.

STEVE: I don't understand; why?

THEODORA: The homosexual men competed for trade with the prostitutes.

STEVE: Well, perhaps we'd better change the subject. What would you say was the chief daily business of a typical Roman Emperor such as Justinian?

THEODORA: *(She thinks briefly.)* War.

STEVE: Really?

THEODORA Yes. He did not—thank God—have the sort of confrontations that you call world wars in your day.

JEFFERSON: I should imagine that the only thing preventing them was lack of suitable transportation and communication.

THEODORA: I'm sure. But the Roman Empire was so vast, you see, that there was scarcely ever a time that one of its subjugated tribes was not in revolt. The Samaritans, who lived in northern Judea, in 528 rebelled and took to arms. We had to kill over a hundred thousand of them to restore peace!

And if once-conquered provinces were not rising there was trouble with powerful neighboring states. Persia presented a dreadfully serious problem.

AUGUSTINE: Tragic, tragic.

STEVE: How did you feel about war, Father?

AUGUSTINE: Depressed. Isn't that how everyone feels about war?

Every war—without exception—is cruel, destructive to the innocent, a product of sinful lusts, and leads to the most insane displays of pomp and supposed glory.

JEFFERSON: Yes. Some of the early church Fathers, you know—Origen and Tertullian, for example—were pacifists.

STEVE: Is that right?

AUGUSTINE: I was not. A great deal depends, you see, on the causes for which men undertake wars. And on the authority they have for doing so. The natural order—which seeks the peace of mankind—ordains that a ruler does have the right to wage war, if he thinks it advisable.

JEFFERSON: You would not argue that all wars are justified.

AUGUSTINE: Oh, certainly not. But some are. Your American Revolutionary War, Mr. President, you would naturally describe as justified.

JEFFERSON: Of course.

THEODORA: All defensive wars are just, are they not, Father?

AUGUSTINE: Of course. A government may certainly repel a hostile force.

STEVE: I suppose the moral problem becomes more difficult when we discuss offensive wars, attacks upon other states.

AUGUSTINE: Indeed. Many offensive wars are *totally* unjustified. But they may be just if the state warred upon has failed either to make reparation for an injurious action committed by its citizens, or if it has failed to return what has been wrongfully appropriated.

RUSSELL: A line of argument that would be appealing to the various terrorist forces in today's world.

THEODORA: And the Imperialist wars of the Roman Empire?

AUGUSTINE: Wars undertaken for the selfish aggrandisement of any empire—whether Roman—British—or American—are not justified. They are immoral!

THEODORA: In your opinion, Father. Has it occurred to you that without the wars of Imperial Rome, Constantine would not have been able to impose Christianity on most of the known world?

AUGUSTINE: Yes. But what is absolutely deplorable about even just wars is the terrible attitude of joyousness and vengefulness its soldiers or citizens may manifest.

Anyone who really thinks in a realistic way on the great evils of war—so horrible, so ruthless—will acknowledge that what war produces is the most dreadful misery.

And if anyone either endures or thinks of such things without mental pain, his is a more miserable plight still, for he thinks himself happy because he has lost all human feeling!

JEFFERSON: Well said, my friend.

AUGUSTINE: But man must, nevertheless, obey the orders of the state.

RUSSELL: Nonsense! Obey Nero? Stalin? Obey Hitler? Are you justifying Dachau? Buchenvald?!

JEFFERSON: One of the wisest things ever said by Jesus, my friend, was that we may know things by their fruits. And when, Father, we regard the effects which your policy of subservience to the state has produced, we are impressed at once by its largely calamitous influence.

RUSSELL: Yes! It is perhaps no historical accident or coincidence that it has been in Germany where this particular Augustinian idea has taken deepest root and brought forth its most poisonous flowers. Long before Hitler, German philosophers were teaching that the high moral ideal of national honor enshrined something positively sacred: something that compelled the individual to sacrifice himself to it.

AUGUSTINE: It is not fair to blame me, gentlemen, for distortions of my teaching! You are being quite unfair. I did indeed say that man should be meek before the might of the state since all power does come from God, but—

RUSSELL: The power of such tyrants as Hitler and Stalin did not come from God!

AUGUSTINE: Whether it did or did not is irrelevant in the context of the point I am making, which is that there is a difference between peaceful submission to the demands of the state on the *one* hand and enthusiastic moral approval of it on the other! I was never guilty of advocating the latter, as you know perfectly well.

RUSSELL: Then it's all the same—so far as results are concerned—if the six million Jews of Europe were killed by men who were only "peacefully submitting" to Hitler's orders!!

AUGUSTINE: My friends Lord Russell and President Jefferson are quite right in suggesting that in judging any philosophy we should always consider its practical results.

They are also correct in feeling that the record of history, over the past two-thousand years, reveals countless shameful acts perpetrated by Christians. Wars, slaughters, terror, corruption—it is all shameful enough, and it is an affront to the ideal of truth to deny that it has occurred. But our distinguished philosophers overlook a very important point.

JEFFERSON: Do we indeed, Father?

AUGUSTINE: I honestly believe so. There is a tendency to consider the record of history as somehow representative—somehow a distillation—of *all* the human acts performed during the period in question. In reality this is not the case. *(To audience)* Our history books are in one regard much like your newspapers or television news reports of the wondrous modern age, which is to say that the record concerns chiefly the *bad* news, which is always—alas—dramatic and colorful, whereas it overlooks the good news.

A man murders a member of his family, for example, and the tragic fact finds its way into the public record. But on the same day the deed was perpetrated, a million families lived in the same community in peace and love.

JEFFERSON: Ah, yes. A very important point.

AUGUSTINE: In assessing the results, in practice, of the Christian philosophy, therefore, we should by no means limit ourselves to the crimes and follies perpetrated by some Christians, but should consider the countless unknown instances of personal decency, courage, virtue. The millions of parents who have tried to bring up their children in love and moral instruction. The couples who have sustained each other with mutual love and support. The heroic sacrifices of individual Christians who have dedicated their lives to the service of God and humankind. These kindly acts—as I say— rarely come to public attention, but they also must be credited to Christianity's account.

STEVE: Reading history is sometimes a sad exercise. All those noble philosophies. All that heroism. All those good intentions, and yet so much tragedy.

AUGUSTINE: This world is a vale of tears, my friend, in which we prepare for a better one.

RUSSELL: Oh, Augustine, don't try to pass off this nice-Nellyism on us. You personally believed most humans are going to spend eternity in the literal flames of Hell!

AUGUSTINE: Now, see here!

STEVE: Gentlemen—uh—Mr. President, may I point something out to those of our audience who may not have had the pleasure of visiting the Jefferson Monument in Washington? These words of our guest are there inscribed: "I have sworn, upon the altar of God, eternal hostility against every form of tyranny over the minds of men."

JEFFERSON: Thank you, sir. That sentiment, of course, pointed to one of the major reasons for our setting up a new country. History till then, as we've just been reminded, had been an endless parade of tyrannies. The pattern had always been the same—a small group seeking control, and manipulating the masses in order that that small party might acquire power and wealth.

Those of us who set up our American charter of human rights hoped—perhaps with more idealism than realism—that we could build a better world. Here on earth, Augustine.

RUSSELL: And you did, my friend, at least in many ways.

STEVE: Mr. President, what would you say were the factors that chiefly distinguished the American experiment from the general patterns that had emerged in the history of the European nations?

JEFFERSON: Well, first . . . one of our most important rights—or freedoms—is the right of nonconformity. This sort of thing was always strongly discouraged in Europe, sad to say, often because of religious bias. Millions of innocent men, women, and children—

you see—since the introduction of Christianity, have been burned, tortured, fined, imprisoned. Yet we do not advance one inch toward uniformity. What has been the effect of such coercion? To make one half the world fools, and the other half hypocrites.

THEODORA: Those are strong words, Mr. Jefferson.

JEFFERSON: Yes, Your Majesty, they have frequently been so described. But the churches must understand that unless there is freedom for heretics, then there cannot possibly be freedom for the churches, for one man's faith is another man's heresy.

As for myself, it does me no injury whatever for my neighbor to say that there are twenty gods—or no god. It neither picks my pocket nor breaks my leg.

STEVE: So you, Mr. President, the political figure, wrote on religion, and, *(turning to Augustine)* an important part of your writings, Father, dealt with political subject matter.

AUGUSTINE: I did indeed deal with political questions, but generally only insofar as they give rise to moral questions. For example, I argued that it was perfectly permissible—if I may return to the point—for a government to be coercive.

STEVE: Really? Why?

AUGUSTINE: Because man is an inherently sinful creature. In other words, it would not be necessary for governments to be coercive if all men were angels, or if they all behaved in a saintly manner at all times. But they do not.

RUSSELL: Except from the anarchist position, there is really nothing to argue about here. Practically everyone agrees that government must be, to a degree, coercive. The important question, of course, concerns that of degree.

Most people, again, would consider the governments ruled by Hitler or Stalin too coercive. But, I am amused, Mr. Allen, that you—in your capacity as an American citizen—have manifested such tolerance in your questioning of Augustine on such matters as freedom and church-state relationships.

STEVE: And why does that amuse you?

RUSSELL: Because there is an absolute contradiction between many of the views of Augustine on these questions and those of the American Founding Fathers.

AUGUSTINE: Lord Russell is absolutely right about this. It is the American view that separation of church and state is an absolute necessity; whereas I felt that the ideal was cooperation between church and state.

JEFFERSON: That is obviously out of the question when Americans belong to thousands of separate churches and sects. *(To Steve)* Augustine's view on this question is indeed—to use a word favored by American conservatives—very un-American.

STEVE: The other area in which you suggested Augustine differed from the American Founding Fathers was—?

RUSSELL: Freedom.

THEODORA: But see here, gentlemen—the freedoms that you Americans consider the norm are not so regarded, even now, by the majority of the inhabitants of the earth. And they have certainly not been so regarded down through history, with very few exceptions.

STEVE: In other words, it is we Americans who are out of step with the march of history as regards the basic freedoms—to speak, to write, to assemble, to vote, and so forth?

THEODORA: Quite so.

RUSSELL: Therefore—to use a concept from economics—your freedoms are indeed precious partly because they are in short supply.

But we should not let Augustine escape so easily from the censure of you Americans for I am afraid you will have learned very little if you let us pass this crucially important point with nothing more than a typically gracious concession by the learned doctor. You see, because Augustine was such an utterly charming fellow, his natural and compassionate instincts initially inclined him to tolerance as regards those whose views differed from his own. But the pressure of public events in time demonstrated that he was, like most lesser men, perfectly capable of sacrificing his good intentions and taking more expedient—and in my view more dangerous—positions.

THEODORA: Dangerous? In what sense?

RUSSELL: Well, literally dangerous to the heretics of his time, Your Majesty.

AUGUSTINE: Lord Russell is quite right in observing that originally my opinion was that no one should be coerced into the unity of Christ—that we Christians must act only by words, fight only by argument, and prevail by force of reason.

JEFFERSON: That certainly hasn't been a very popular view among churchmen over the past five thousand years.

AUGUSTINE: No. But after some years of experience it occurred to me that if the state has the power to punish the poisoning of the body it must also have the power to punish the poisoning of the mind.

STEVE: Yes, that's quite interesting, Father. It's precisely the argument that Thomas Aquinas used—when he visited us—to justify the burning of heretics at the stake.

RUSSELL: Ah, capital, capital! Again, we must always examine the concrete, specific results of our philosophical beliefs, if we are to fully understand them, for many a proposition which seems harmless enough when considered in the abstract can lead to the most hideous reality.

JEFFERSON: As Jesus said, "By their fruits you will know them."

AUGUSTINE: I hope no one will assume that I drew my views out of thin air! There was scriptural justification for them.

RUSSELL: I am not surprised.

AUGUSTINE: *(Ignoring the thrust)* In Luke, Chapter 14, verses 21 to 24, we find the story of the master whose invited guests do not come to his banquet, and who therefore sends his servant out to compel strangers to come in.

RUSSELL: Oh, really! I ask everyone—at least those whose critical faculties are not simply numbed by the Scriptures—to ask how they personally would feel if they were walking down the street one day and the servant of an important man, or public official, actually forced them to attend a dinner when they personally wished to be about other business. There isn't a person listening to us right now who would not be very much offended. And yet we are presumably to approve of such conduct for one reason and one reason alone: that it is spoken of respectfully in the Bible.

STEVE: Your Majesty—gentlemen—I'm sorry to say we're out of time. May I be assured that all of you will join us again next time to continue this fascinating discussion?

ALL: *(Ad lib their willingness to return.)*

STEVE: Very well. Thank you.

And thank you for having joined us for this Meeting of Minds. Do be back with us for our next program.

SHOW # 14

St. Augustine of Hippo
(IVOR FRANCIS)

*The Empress Theodora
of the Byzantine Empire*
(SALOME JENS)

Thomas Jefferson
(SHEPPERD STRUDWICK)

Bertrand Russell
(JOHN HOYT)

Welcome to another Meeting of Minds. Returning for a continua-
tion of their earlier discussion, our guests this evening are:
    From fourth-century Africa . . . St. Augustine of Hippo.
    From sixth-century Constantinople . . . the Empress Theodora.
    From eighteenth-century America . . . President Thomas
Jefferson.
    And from twentieth-century England . . . Lord Bertrand Russell.
    And now . . . your host, Steve Allen.
STEVE: Thank you. In speaking with Lord Russell last time, we found
    him to be a genial unbeliever, but one with certain almost Chris-
    tian views. Lord Russell would have us look to reason and science,
    however, for our salvation.
        St. Augustine, of course, takes a very different view.
        From Empress Theodora we learned of her impoverished, even
    scandalous, background.
        Thomas Jefferson is seen—by American eyes—in such a heroic
    light that we tend to think of him as the enormous figure on Mt.
    Rushmore, more like a god than a human being. What, then, can
    we accurately say of Thomas Jefferson? That he deserves the mantle
    of greatness with which time, and American bias, have clothed
    him. . . . *(He approaches the table.)* Well, hopefully this evening
    we shall come to know more of the *real* Thomas Jefferson.
RUSSELL: Quite so! Mr. Allen, I wonder if you, as an American citizen,
    are aware that your third president was also an inventor?
STEVE: No, I didn't know that. What did you invent, Mr. President?
JEFFERSON: Oh, a number of things. An adjustable desk, a portable
    copying machine, a plow, a central heating system, a swivel chair.
STEVE: My goodness. Did you make much money from your inventions?
JEFFERSON: I was lucky enough to be blessed by nature with a number
    of gifts, sir, but a gift for the earning of money—or the management
    of it—was not among them. I conducted my own financial affairs
    so poorly, in fact, that when I died I was very close to bankruptcy.
    But, you know, my friends, I absolutely revel in the idea that I
    can speak my mind freely here and not have to worry about
    consequences, except those dictated by my own conscious.
STEVE: I don't quite follow you, Mr. President.
JEFFERSON: Well, you see, in my lifetime I was frequently attacked
    by a press that was hostile, in some cases even vicious.
STEVE: That's hard for us modern Americans to grasp. Practically no
    one criticizes you now. But, is that perhaps why you published
    so little in the way of political philosophy?

JEFFERSON: Absolutely. I tried to make as small a target of myself as possible.

STEVE: I wonder what it was, Mr. President, that provided the source of your creative energy, your fervor.

JEFFERSON: Perhaps it was nothing more, Mr. Allen, than my familiarity with the realities of political life in Europe. I knew something of Europe's history, of course, and except for the scholars of the Enlightenment, the whole continent seemed to have learned nothing. Through the years I spent in Europe I often amused myself with contemplating the characters of the then-reigning sovereigns.

STEVE: What sort of people were they?

JEFFERSON: Well, Louis XVI was a fool . . . the King of Spain was a fool, and of Naples the same.

STEVE: Really. . . .

JEFFERSON: Yes, they passed their lives in hunting. . . . The King of Sardinia was a fool. . . . The Queen of Portugal . . . was an idiot by nature. And so was the King of Denmark. . . . The King of Prussia, successor to the great Frederick, was a mere hog in body as well as in mind. Gustavus of Sweden and Joseph of Austria were really crazy, and George of England . . . was in a straight-jacket. . . .

To sum up, I was determined that we would avoid the dreadful mistakes made by the Europeans. I wrote to James Monroe in 1785 that a trip to Europe would make him absolutely adore his own country. My God, how little do my countrymen know what precious blessings they are in possession of, which no other people on earth enjoy!

STEVE: Mr. President, your own life was so full of activity and creation, I doubt that you spent much time looking on the dark, pessimistic side of life.

JEFFERSON: Of course not. And for all those who do spend time thinking about such dreary things as the possible *end* of the world, well, let me give them a little advice. Be prepared for it, and the best way to do that is to lead a good life. If ever you are *about* to say anything amiss, or to do something wrong, consider before-hand. You will feel something within you which will tell you it is wrong, and ought not to be said or done. This is your con-science. Be sure to obey it. Our Maker has given us all this faith-ful internal monitor; and if you always obey it, you will always be prepared for the end of the world; or for a much more certain event, which is death.

This must happen to us all; it puts an end to the world as to us, and the best way to be ready for it is never to do a wrong act.

AUGUSTINE: *(With a smile)* Mr. President, you've said in a few moments what some priests have taken a lifetime to say.

RUSSELL: Yes, but I wish humankind had by now developed in intelligence to the point where it wouldn't be necessary to wave a stick in its face and say "be good."

THEODORA: Do you see any alternative?

RUSSELL: Certainly! Science! Reason! Religion is based, I think, primarily on fear. It is partly the understandable terror of the unknown, and partly the wish to feel that you have a kind of elder brother who will stand by you in your troubles and disputes. Fear is the basis of the whole thing! Fear of the mysterious, fear of defeat, fear of death.

THEODORA: If you had lived in my time and place, Russell, I could have taught you fear!

RUSSELL: I have little doubt of that, Your Majesty. You were quite prepared to order the death of those who displeased you. But that would be reasonable fear. I refer to unreasonable fear. And science can help us get over this craven fear in which mankind has lived for so many centuries. Science can teach us, and I think our own hearts can teach us, no longer to look for imaginary supports, no longer to invent allies in the sky, but rather to look to our own efforts here below to make this world a fit place to live in, instead of the sort of place that the churches in all these centuries have made it.

AUGUSTINE: Russell, you have no right to assume that almost everyone has your kind of intellect and is capable of your kind of self-comforting rationality! Your brain is a gift of God and you should use it for His purposes! One of those purposes should be encouraging mankind to have faith.

RUSSELL: My friend, people who feel they must have a faith in order to face life are showing a kind of cowardice, which in any other sphere would be considered contemptible. But when it is in the *religious* sphere it is thought admirable. I cannot admire cowardice, whatever sphere it is in.

THEODORA: Peace, gentlemen, peace! Let us change the subject. Er—Mr. Jefferson, I'm curious about your early years.

JEFFERSON: Well, I was born in comfortable circumstances, Your Majesty, so in a sense I'm not a good example of the American Dream.

I didn't have to struggle, you see. I was born on my father's estate, Shadwell, in Albemarle County, Virginia, in April of 1743.

STEVE: What did your father do?

JEFFERSON: He was a civil engineer who became a justice of the peace and, eventually, a member of the House of Burgesses, which was the legislature of Virginia. He was also something of a freethinker.

STEVE: And your mother?

JEFFERSON: She was a member of one of the most prominent colonial families, the Randolphs.

AUGUSTINE: How did you become politically prominent?

JEFFERSON: Again, circumstances, Father. At sixteen I entered William and Mary College at Williamsburg where I became a good student. I loved academic life and the mental stimulation, and I became associated with some very interesting gentlemen, one of them being George Wythe, who was a leading member of the Virginia bar and a great scholar.

In college I studied languages, natural sciences, and mathematics— I really enjoyed all these things, although I dropped out at the age of nineteen.

Afterwards I joined Wythe's law office. I was admitted to the bar in 1767 and practiced law for seven years.

STEVE: You must have enjoyed that!

JEFFERSON: No, Mr. Allen. I found that being a lawyer was not entirely to my taste. I wanted something more.

STEVE: More, really?

JEFFERSON: But the law as a profession was beginning to change— to expand its philosophical horizons.

STEVE: In what way?

JEFFERSON: Those of us engaged in law at that time gradually came to see the profession as being far more than a money-making occupation. It seemed to us that it could be a powerful force in shaping the institutions and the culture of our people! And therefore a potent instrument for social reform.

STEVE: You must have enjoyed speaking out your great ideas, Mr. President!

JEFFERSON: Oh, not at all, sir! I very much *dis*liked making speeches.

STEVE: Really?

JEFFERSON: Yes! Prior to the outbreak of the war with England, I don't recall that I ever made one!

STEVE: But in those exciting debates about the prospects for revolution and freedom you—

JEFFERSON: Oh, I hated debate! I once coined the phrase "the morbid rage of debate" because it seemed to me that men are never really convinced by such argumentation. They are more convinced by reading and by reflection.

AUGUSTINE: Perhaps they should be, Mr. Jefferson, but I devoted much of my life to debate against heretics.

JEFFERSON: Indeed, Father, I loved good, provocative conversation. In fact, if any of you had been guests at Monticello you would likely have done just what we're doing now.

STEVE: But, you must have found the time for solitude. Is it true that you wrote a total of some eighteen thousand letters!?

JEFFERSON: Yes.

THEODORA: With so busy a pen you must also have written a great many books.

JEFFERSON: Only one, Your Majesty, *Notes on Virginia,* and I did not originally see it as a *book* at all.

STEVE: But what about the book people call "Jefferson's Bible"?

JEFFERSON: That consisted, Mr. Allen, of the sayings of Jesus, without the additions by others, such as St. Paul. Strange to say, many Christians seem to give as much weight to the statements of Paul as they do to those of Jesus himself.

STEVE: I see. Well, you had started to tell us of your political background.

JEFFERSON: Yes. My political life began in 1769—I was then twenty-six—when I took a seat in the House of Burgesses, the lower house of the colonial legislature—and held it until I was sent by Virginia as a delegate to the Continental Congress in Philadelphia, in 1775. Things moved very fast—I was prominent in the deliberative bodies—it was a time of revolution, a marvelous moment in history to be alive! Think of it! To be a part of a completely new concept in self-government! New laws and institutions—Republicanism instead of government by a distant parliament and an unreasonable king.

It was not an easy time, of course, and there were many moments when it looked as if our cause was lost. But I considered myself fortunate to have been part of it all.

STEVE: Mr. President, how can the United States always keep precisely the form of government which you and your friends devised for us?

JEFFERSON: What? Sir, I considered that a *very* strange question! I am obviously biased in favor of such government, and I hope that it will never be lightly cast aside, but each generation has the right

to choose for itself the form of government it believes is promotive
of its own happiness.

Our Constitution is important, and it has been a great protector
of the freedoms of the people, but there is this dreadful tendency—
that may fairly be described as stupid—this tendency to ascribe
to the men of a preceding age a wisdom more than human, and
consequently to imagine that whatever was done in ancient times
must be beyond amendment or improvement.

RUSSELL: Good for you, Jefferson!

JEFFERSON: This is a very foolish way to look at things. Laws and
constitutions must go hand-in-hand with the progress of the human mind. New discoveries are made, new *truths* disclosed, and
new problems present themselves. The laws, and forms of
government, must keep abreast of these changes.

STEVE: I see. You know, Mr. President, in more dignified or conservative times, the aura of scandal attached to the Empress Theodora's
name, if you'll forgive me Your Majesty, would have caused most
people to regard her with strong moral disapproval. Does it in
any way depress you, sir, as one of the idealistic creators of our
American society, that not only does Theodora today tend to be
viewed in somewhat glamorous terms, but that even many living
Americans seem to be greatly admired and envied, *despite* their
scandalous lives, as long as they are successsful?

JEFFERSON: Yes. It saddens me greatly. It is an extremely dangerous
situation for our society when criminality or indencency are
considered praiseworthy or amusing, and decency is held in *low*
regard. Our nation was founded in a burst of idealistic energy.
We were able to look back at the terrible price Europe had paid
for tyranny, for corruption, and we wished to avoid such errors,
or at least to diminish them.

AUGUSTINE: Mankind will truly reform itself, my friends, only by the
grace of God, not by the advice of emperors or presidents.

JEFFERSON: Then why does our Maker withhold such a blessing, sir?

AUGUSTINE: *(With a sigh)* I do not know.

RUSSELL: Nor does anyone else, my friend. Plato observed—in the
Timaeus—that "the maker of this universe is past finding out." Now
surely here, sir, is an assertion in which all believers and nonbe-
lievers can find agreement.

AUGUSTINE: But we proceed to add, your Lordship, that since philosophy, unaided, *cannot* lead them to God—at least with any

sense of certainty—we must therefore turn to revelation for our certainty.

RUSSELL: Not again! Had it been established to the satisfaction of all mankind, Augustine, that there was such a thing as divine revelation, your argument would be unassailable. But that is precisely the point on which your entire argument stands or falls.

THEODORA: By *revelation* you mean, of course, Father—

AUGUSTINE: The record of the Old and New Testaments—

RUSSELL: Precisely. And surely you must know that even among extremely devout Christians and Jewish Bible scholars of the present age, there is the most incredible diversity of opinion about literally thousands of specific Bible references.

You, Your Majesty, were a Monophysite Christian. You differed with Augustine in believing that Christ had only one nature.

THEODORA: *(Angrily)* The Bible clearly says that the Son—

RUSSELL: The Bible, Your Majesty, is noted for a number of virtues. Clarity is *not* one of them! The Scriptures are, in fact, the most incredible hodge-podge of factual inaccuracy, internal contradiction, and atrocity represented as divinely authorized, as well as crimes defended simply because they were committed by men who—it was already decided—were holy.

THEODORA: How dare you, sir!

RUSSELL: *(To Augustine)* Far from winning the day, my friend, by moving the argument out of the domain of reason to that of revelation, the religious believer rather ensures his defeat, at least to the satisfaction of men and women of intelligence who have taken the trouble to study the Scriptures.

If we assume—for purposes of argumentation—that there is in fact an all-good, all-wise, all-loving God, then I argue that to assert that such a Divine entity is the primary author of so atrocious a literary record as the Bible is the worst conceivable insult to the Deity.

THEODORA: Disgraceful!

JEFFERSON: Hear, hear!

RUSSELL: Indeed it has for long years been profoundly puzzling to me as to how intelligent individuals—many of them personally virtuous and well-intentioned—could possibly worship a being morally inferior to themselves!

THEODORA: God is the Supreme Being, sir! Supreme in every way. All-powerful. All-good. How could you possibly be so wicked as to hate an all-loving—?

RUSSELL: See here, Your Majesty, I do not hate God! Only an insane person would hate God. I simply cannot see any evidence that such a personage exists.

AUGUSTINE: He existed before the heavens and the earth!

RUSSELL: *(Smiling)* I wonder if you can tell us, Father, precisely what God was doing *before* He made heaven and earth?

AUGUSTINE: *(With a wry smile)* He was preparing Hell for pryers into mysteries! In all seriousness, my friend, He was not doing anything at all, because if He had been doing anything we would have to assume that He was creating.

RUSSELL: Ah, assume, assume! Do you concede, Father, that there is—once again—something here that you supernaturalists simply cannot explain, for your line of argument leads us to think of a time before time began, which is a contradiction in terms?

AUGUSTINE: Yes. *(He sighs.)* There is a great deal the believer cannot explain.

THEODORA: *(Shocked)* What?!

AUGUSTINE: But—there is even more the unbeliever cannot explain.

THEODORA: Good!

JEFFERSON: A clever turn of phrase, learned doctor, but the area that the unbelievers *can* explain grows daily, while you priests are never able to probe one inch farther into your realms of mystery than you were countless thousands of years ago, at the beginnings of your speculation!

THEODORA: Your Lordship, do you perceive *anything* of value in Christianity at all?

RUSSELL: Oh, most assuredly, Your Majesty. There is nothing human or natural that is totally evil, as Shakespeare suggested when he observed that it is a remarkably evil wind that blows no good whatever. And there are many charming and virtuous people who are Christians, though I suspect they are simply nice by nature. And I have always found that element of Christian philosophy attractive which was most humble.

You yourself, Augustine, admired Plato, and Plotinus, among the ancients. And, you know, Neoplatonism was a rather appealing form of Christianity, so far as its negative theology was concerned.

STEVE: Could you make that clearer, Lord Russell?

RUSSELL: Certainly. The negative theology of which I speak declared that all we can truly know about God is what He is not, and that we have *no* way whatever of knowing what He *is*. I find the humility here rather endearing.

AUGUSTINE: Even if we cannot know what God *is,* Russell, we do know what He *does.*

RUSSELL: You do not in fact, know any such thing, my friend. You observe what is done—and then you simply assume something about a force powerful enough to do it! But even among the most intelligent Christians over the centuries—philosophers such as yourself, sir, Origen, Clement of Alexandria, Nicholas of Cusa, Abelard, Eusebius, John Scotus Erigena, Aquinas—among all of you, as I say, we find the most heated disagreement—repeatedly—on dozens of important questions.

STEVE: Such as?

RUSSELL: Well, as for Origen, who was one of the fathers of the Church, he differed with Augustine on the question of predestination. And, Origen believed in a successive variety of worlds. He believed, in other words, in reincarnation.

STEVE: Really?

RUSSELL: Yes! He felt that the body must somehow be refined or spiritualized before man could be saved, and consequently that the soul must live—again and again—through many bodies, and perhaps many worlds, before it would be pure enough to return to its heavenly home. Now your Christian churches at the present moment are firmly of the opinion that such a belief is utter nonsense. It is considered now—by Christians—a degraded, pagan, inferior, Oriental notion.

And yet if Origen were here at this table—*(He turns to Steve.)* as, may I recommend, he may someday be—he would defend such a view, with no doubt as much creativity and sense of certainty as you are displaying yourself, Augustine. But is there anybody in this audience today who believes in reincarnation? *(Several people in audience applaud.)*

(To one woman) You believe in reincarnation? *(Pause. He nods.)* Welcome back!

But Augustine, my friend, before you Christians can convincingly address the world—or at least the more intelligent of its inhabitants—you must get your own houses in philosophical order. It is pointless to say to the world, "Christianity is the answer" when— I repeat—there are a thousand and one *forms* of Christianity.

JEFFERSON: Yes, and when, moreover, some of these forms have been literally at war with others over the centuries, not hesitating to resort to the arrow, the spear, the sword, poison, the machinery of torture, and the hideous fires of the stake in alleged defense of a loving Christ and a merciful God.

THEODORA: Heresy, Mr. President, must be stamped out, and vigorously, in defense of Christian truth!

JEFFERSON: Your Majesty, you have just agreed to your own death warrant. For in Augustine's opinion you were a heretic!

RUSSELL: You asked me a moment ago, Augustine, what in Christianity I find admirable. It has just occurred to me that another endearing habit of Christians is their tendency to throw themselves on their knees while praying. It is no wonder that Christians spend a certain amount of time on their knees. The wonder is rather that they ever have the temerity to stand up, considering their historical record.

For surely you must be aware—to your own sorrow, Father—that the record of Christian history is far more than that of the New Testament, far more than the writings of such distinguished and charming philosophers as yourself, far more than the edifying lives of a handful of saints. It is also the record of what vast armies of Christians have done—in their formal capacities as Christians—down through the centuries.

Jesus was very wise in suggesting that we may know things by their fruits, which is to say, their results. Ideas—as it has been said—have consequences, and I would think that every Christian scholar would shudder at contemplation of many of the consequences of Christian philosophy in the world.

AUGUSTINE: Russell, if an Englishmen becomes a murderer, is his crime the fault of all England? Mr. Jefferson, if an American is corrupt or otherwise evil, is his sin to be blamed on you and the other American Founding Fathers, or your philosophy?

As for Christianity, Lord Russell, it has achieved true glories and produced many blessings!

RUSSELL: Beyond any doubt, my friend. But if anyone imagines that is all it has produced, he is very much mistaken, and moreover has the moral obligation to examine the full—not just the partial—historical record. Why, you Christians even approved of slavery for centuries. You personally, Augustine, said that the slave must be subject to his master.

JEFFERSON: Yes, and I regret to say that those of us who wished to *abolish* slavery were very bitterly attacked by the churches for our efforts.

AUGUSTINE: You know, Mr. Russell, although the great Thomas Aquinas would differ with me, there's a certain sense in which the Christian—

and perhaps the believer in any form of religious philosophy—will always be at a disadvantage in argumentation with the pure rationalist such as yourself.

JEFFERSON: I have perceived the disadvantage, Father, but am curious to know if you and Lord Russell would agree on a definition of it.

AUGUSTINE: *(He smiles.)* I refer, Mr. President, to the fact that though we ought to follow reason to its uttermost limits, and never speak of it contemptuously, there is—nevertheless—a portion of that realm encompassed by religious belief that exists outside the boundaries of reason. Again, though Aquinas would disagree, I personally concede for example, that by purely rational standards the existence of God cannot be satisfactorily demonstrated.

THEODORA: What?!

AUGUSTINE: This in no way weakens my own faith in God, Your Majesty, needless to say. I am merely making a concession required by the standards of reason itself. But the rationalist defines the terms of the classic debate in such a way that, as I say, the religious believer must ultimately fail to satisfy the rationalist's requirements.

RUSSELL: Your concession is graceful, Father. I would add only that when the believer has been forced—by the requirements of reason— to a position where his back is against the wall—he simply solves his dilemma, to his *own* satisfaction at least, by leaping *over* the wall and proclaiming that he now stands in a territory where reason cannot follow.

THEODORA: Do you deny, sir, that anything *exists* on the other side of that wall?

RUSSELL: I see no evidence of it, Your Majesty.

AUGUSTINE: Would you perhaps agree, gentlemen, that—while reason cannot determine which of a thousand conflicting religious forms is truly of God, that reason can nevertheless at least determine which is the best, the most worthy of an intelligent individual's respect?

RUSSELL: Oh, yes.

JEFFERSON: Perhaps your question arises out of the assumption that a rational analysis of the claims of rival religions would lead to the conclusion that, as you might say, the Roman Catholic form is superior.

AUGUSTINE: But of course.

JEFFERSON: I would observe only that millions of devout Christians would disagree with you.

RUSSELL: But more importantly, even if Roman Catholicism were the best of all the forms of religion, this would have nothing whatever to do with the question as to whether it was valid. In a series of philosophical mish-moshes, that one which is the least offensive may be termed "the best," without actually being valid or true at all.

JEFFERSON: It might be instructive, in this connection, to return to your question, Mr. Allen, about the disunity of Christianity in its *early* centuries. I believe, for example, that modern man should know something of the Arian controversy.

STEVE: Would you object, Father?

AUGUSTINE: Quite the contrary. I agree with Mr. Jefferson on this.

STEVE: Very well. What was Arianism?

AUGUSTINE: The name derives from Arius, a church official of Alexandria who in the year 320 was condemned by his bishop for his heretical views.

STEVE: What were those views?

AUGUSTINE: Arius argued first that God—as the begetter of all things—must Himself be unbegotten. In other words nobody *else* created God.

STEVE: That seems reasonable enough.

THEODORA: But Arius proceeded from this reasonable assumption to argue that anything that was created—such as Jesus, the Son of God—or Logos—or Wisdom—must, by definition, occupy a position inferior to that of God.

STEVE: Ah, I see. And it was the more common Christian belief that Jesus was literally equal to God, in all respects.

RUSSELL: It must sadden you now, Father Augustine—and you, Your Majesty—to observe that there are millions of Christians, and others, who agree with Arius on this point.

AUGUSTINE: *(Somberly)* It saddens me greatly.

JEFFERSON: Arius was opposed by a man named Athanasius, who argued the view that is now part of Catholic dogma, as well as that of some of the Protestant divisions. Athanasius argued not only that Christ was simply God in human form, but that a third personal entity—the Holy Spirit, or Holy Ghost—was *also* God. Equal, that is, to the other two.

RUSSELL: Precisely. To most people this adds up to three gods. But it did *not* to Athanasius.

JEFFERSON: Arianism, in fact, has been called by one modern scholar the heresy of common sense.

RUSSELL: *(Chuckles)* Quite so.

JEFFERSON: And the Arians, you know, believed that they had the Old Testament on their side.

STEVE: Really? In what sense?

RUSSELL: Well, in the Old Testament the prophets—or whoever it was who actually wrote those books—were *very* insistent on the idea of monotheism, which is to say the idea of one God.

THEODORA: This was in contrast to many pagan faiths—such as those of the Greeks and Romans—which were prepared to accept the idea that there were numerous gods.

RUSSELL: Yes. The Arians were horrified by this polytheism, and believed that they were opposing it in insisting that there was only one god, instead of the three that common sense tells us the Athanasians believed in.

JEFFERSON: In any event, a good many un-Christian things were done and said in the heat of the controversy, and in time the followers of Athanasius—including the learned Augustine—carried the day.

STEVE: Well, thank you for giving us this background information. Would it be correct, Father, to say that the great bulk of your writing—and you have left behind an enormous volume of work— that the great bulk of it was written in the heat of such controversy?

AUGUSTINE: Yes, that is correct. I attempted—in every possible way— to demonstrate that the way of the good and blessed life is to be found entirely in the *true* religion.

STEVE: Which is—?

AUGUSTINE: The one wherein one God is worshipped and acknowledged to be the beginning of all existing things. Thus, you see, it becomes easy to detect the error of those who have preferred to worship many gods, because their wise men—whom they call philosophers— used to have various schools, all in disagreement with one another, although they made common use of the temples.

STEVE: Yes. It's occurred to me as odd that the pagans could boast of the greatest, most brilliant philosophers—Socrates, Plato, Aristotle, and the rest—and yet their religion was—it's safe to say it now, thousands of years later—really stupid.

JEFFERSON: *(He laughs.)* Before commenting on your point, Augustine, let us make quite sure that we grasp what you mean. You are saying that the weakness—the *error*—of the philosophers was not so much that they worshipped many gods—which as our host has observed was a ridiculous form of religion—but rather because their various schools of philosophy were in constant disagreement?

AUGUSTINE: Yes. That is precisely what I mean.

JEFFERSON: Very well. Then you have just offered a remarkably convincing proof of the falsity of the Christian religion.

STEVE: How do you mean?

JEFFERSON: As we look about the world, sir, we see that Lord Russell was right in pointing out the thousands of individual sects and churches, each of which insists that it preaches the best possible sort of Christianity. *(To audience)* It therefore follows that if Augustine is right—as I for one think he is—that there cannot be a number of mutually contradictory versions of the truth—then it inescapably follows there cannot be many mutually contradictory versions of Christianity all equally deserving of our respect.

AUGUSTINE: Far from refuting me, sir, you have—on the contrary— supported me, and as handsomely as I might have done myself.

THEODORA: Good for you, Augustine!

AUGUSTINE: For I agree that reason is scandalized by the existence of a host of rival claimants to ownership of Christian truth. But all that such an argument proves is that there can only be one right form of the Christian faith.

RUSSELL: Ah, that word again! Faith! Father, mankind must eventually realize that it must have the courage to stand on its own two feet and not look vaguely into the skies for help. As for the faith that sustained you, I don't doubt its value in your own case. But faith itself—precisely what *is* it? In the case of faith about something that exists and can be proved, such as chemical formulas, then I see no harm in arriving at an answer and having faith that your answer is correct. But in matters of the abstract and the intangible, faith can be dangerous and harmful! Man's capacity for self-delusion is well documented, and frightening.

STEVE: Well, Lord Russell, to survive in any profession for a long period of time—about seventy years in your own case—requires a considerable strength of mind and spine. What was it that sustained you? What were your beliefs and passions?

RUSSELL: I was maintained by three simple but very strong passions, Mr. Allen. First was the longing for love.

Second was the search for knowledge.

Third, an unbearable pity for the sufferings of mankind.

These passions, like a great wind, blew me hither and thither in a wayward course over a deep ocean of anguish, and at times took me to the very edge of despair.

I sought love, in the first place, because it brings ecstasy, an ecstasy so great that there were times when I would have sacrificed all the rest of life for a few hours of that joy. I also sought love because it relieves loneliness—that terrible loneliness we humans know when our consciousness lets us look out over the rim of the world into the cold, unfathomable lifeless abyss.

AUGUSTINE: An abyss, my friend, inhabited only by God.

RUSSELL: Well. . . . Lastly I sought love because in the union of love I saw, in a mystic miniature, the vision of heaven that saints and poets have imagined. This, in any event, is what I sought, and, though it might seem too good for human life, it is what I finally found.

THEODORA: You speak pretty words, your Lordship, but you were married—how many times?

RUSSELL: Three.

THEODORA: Divorce, for you, was apparently easily achieved. But easy divorce, to me, seems a curse in the modern world! Justinian and I would not allow it! Except when the man or woman wished to enter the religious life.

AUGUSTINE: Yes, divorce is a great evil indeed because it may lead to the abandonment of small children. (To Russell) But I respect your yearning for the bliss of love, my friend. I found it with my two mistresses. But passion may not last. The love of God—and for God—lasts for all eternity! Our Lord Jesus preached love for all. He opened his arms to all mankind!

STEVE: Very few people today seem to feel they've found a true place and purpose in life. Why is modern man so insecure?

AUGUSTINE: The answer is simple. If you believe in God and His divine purposes, you understand that you are a part of life in order to serve Him. If you serve Him well you will find satisfaction. You will respect your fellow man. You will not look with contempt or suspicion on others.

STEVE: May we return to history?

AUGUSTINE: Certainly.

STEVE: During our last discussion we mentioned the bias of Roman Emperor Constantine in favor of Christianity. Perhaps we should clarify that Constantine did not make Christianity the one official religion of the Empire. He did, however, say that it was the religion favored by the Roman state.

AUGUSTINE: Constantine was personally chosen by God to make the Christian faith dominant in the world.

RUSSELL: Augustine, you don't really know that! Why did God wait some four hundred years to choose Constantine? Why didn't He choose Augustus Caesar and save more millions of souls? But Constantine seems to have believed that he was so chosen. This is very important, you see.

STEVE: Why?

RUSSELL: Because Constantine, and those Emperors who followed him, were no longer considered merely the most powerful individuals, whose strength grew from the support of the army, but rather as those who ruled by direct divine sanction!

STEVE: Ah, I see.

THEODORA: Even more importantly, gentlemen, this change meant that the Roman Empire was *now* considered much more than a powerful state.

AUGUSTINE: Quite so. The state was now viewed as part of God's plan for the salvation of mankind.

STEVE: Last time, Father, we had started to discuss the reaction of Roman pagans when the Empire began to crumble.

AUGUSTINE: Yes. When the Goths, under their King Alaric, captured Rome in the summer of the year 410, the shock to the Roman upper classes was very great. The pagans blamed the defeat on Christianity.

RUSSELL: Yes, most people are unaware that the Goths were Christians.

STEVE: Really? Then Gibbon, in his *Decline and Fall of the Roman Empire,* was not the first to advance such a theory.

AUGUSTINE: By no means. But there is small profit in seeking credit for such a theory because its argument was groundless.

It was not the fault of us Christians that Rome had collapsed. In fact, to respond to such arguments, I began to write my *City of God.* I explained that the Roman Empire—like any other— could not possibly last forever, but that it would naturally have its time of power and its time of weakness and decay. I explained that the only permanent social entity would be that of the church— visible and invisible—which I called the "City of God."

STEVE: You know, a factor that emerges from all our conversation here is the perverse nature of man, which has frustrated so many utopian philosophies. You once suggested, Lord Russell, that humankind needs to think in terms of equality in order to feel secure and peaceful. Surely man needs to be more malleable to arrive at that point. But the thing that strikes many people about human nature is that it *isn't* very malleable.

RUSSELL: Oh, I cannot agree at all!

JEFFERSON: Nor can I! Human nature is infinitely perfectable, improvable!

RUSSELL: Of course. If you compared a dog with a wild wolf you will see what training can do. The domestic dog is a nice comfortable creature, whereas the wolf is quite another thing.

Now you can do exactly the same thing with human beings. Human beings, according to how they are treated, will turn out totally different, and I think the idea that you cannot change human nature at all is silly.

AUGUSTINE: Russell, you fail to distinguish between human nature and human behavior!

RUSSELL: Do you concede, my friend, that men can be reformed?

AUGUSTINE: Of course. By taking Christ into their hearts!

RUSSELL: *(With a smile)* Yes, that sometimes occurs. They also do it by taking Mohammed or Buddha into their hearts. Or Karl Marx, for that matter, most unfortunately. But my point is that man's nature can be improved, civilized.

STEVE: Then the question becomes—how?

JEFFERSON: By education!

AUGUSTINE: But not merely the academic kind. We need a realization of the soul, a belief that man is more than an intelligent animal and that he is, in fact, the special, dear creation of God. That, my friends, is where the ideal of human dignity originates.

STEVE: Human dignity. But the terrible truth is that we live in a world still plagued with starvation and people being put to death.

RUSSELL: One of the reasons is overpopulation.

STEVE: Something you warned about many years ago. In fact, I doubt if any philosopher has been more vocal on that subject than yourself.

RUSSELL: And for which I was roundly condemned, though I'm pleased to see that the subject is finally meeting with proper consideration. There are still some, of course, who find the idea of birth control shocking.

AUGUSTINE: I am one of them, sir. We have no right to interfere with one of God's own processes.

RUSSELL: Oh, now you approve of sex? Most of the time you wrote about it as the Devil's handiwork!

THEODORA: Your Lordship, I hardly feel that your own record entitles you to lecture us on the sanctity of marriage.

AUGUSTINE: Good point!

THEODORA: And what about your own early life, Father?

AUGUSTINE: Like yourself, I reformed my sinful ways, Your Majesty.

JEFFERSON: Well, whether we're discussing responsible parenthood, or any other important question, it's refreshing that we can exchange ideas here in complete freedom. It's incredible what dreadful things have been done because people would not permit the free exchange of views. That way lies tyranny.

RUSSELL: It's unavoidable as long as man persists in preventing free inquiry. The purpose of education should be to produce thought, not belief.

STEVE: To teach people how to think, rather than just what to think.

RUSSELL: Precisely! Youngsters are still compelled to hold positive opinions on doubtful matters, rather than let them see the doubtfulness and be encouraged to independence to mind. Education ought to foster the wish for truth, not the conviction that some particular creed is the truth.

JEFFERSON: I agree, but I think it is possible to arrive at a degree of truth. The basic moral tenets of Christianity and Judaism form truth, in my opinion—the Ten Commandments, the Golden Rule. I see no harm in accepting this as a creed by which to live. Surely, if nothing else, the religions help to keep people on the straight and narrow. After all, religions do espouse virtue.

RUSSELL: Yes, but often dangerously so. And your Ten Commandments, Mr. Jefferson—which number far more than ten, by the way (count them sometime)—say that God personally forbids the making of statues. It is not a sin to make a religious statue, as Michelangelo could tell you. But owing to the identification of religion with virtue, together with the fact that the most religious men are usually not the most intelligent—*(To Augustine)* there are exceptions of course—a religious education gives courage to the stupid to resist the authority of educated men, as has happened, for example, where the teaching of evolution has been made illegal.

THEODORA: Gentlemen, you speak eloquently but you deal in supposition. Theory. Life is a minute by minute physical experience. Our bodies dictate our actions even more than our minds. The body has its hungers, and if the hungers are not met, then all your theories are vanities. I doubt if any of you gentlemen have any idea what it is to be really hungry or to be in need of basic shelter.

JEFFERSON: *(With wry humor)* Are we to be criticized because we were not poor?

THEODORA: *(Eyes flashing)* Poverty is no laughing matter, sir! I was a product of poverty. I saw people starve. I saw them die in the gutter. I know what it meant to sell my body for food!

If men had this natural godliness you seem to think they have, Augustine, if all men had your infinite intelligence, Lord Russell, or your nobility, Mr. President, then your lectures might have more impact. But the majority in my day barely made a living.

(To Steve) And you can boast of science and reason in your modern world, but half the population of this earth even now is living on a bare subsistence level. Life is still desperate and yet you idly talk.

JEFFERSON: You are right, Your Majesty. But it is through talk that we communicate, that we make decisions, discover the means of righting wrongs. We must talk. We must question.

THEODORA: *(Resignedly)* Well, mine was a more practical life, so you'll pardon my skepticism.

STEVE: We'd like to know more about that life, Your Majesty. You told us last time about your marriage to Justinian and how, later, in the year 527, he became Emperor and yourself Empress of the Byzantine world. Again, what manner of man was Justinian?

THEODORA: He had a good mind but rather opulent sensual tastes. Part of the colorful character of Byzantine art stems from his own tastes, you know. He loved glitter and color, though he ate very simple food and did not drink. He was a scholarly man, and gave the impression of being somewhat aloof. But, he loved to surround himself with grandeur whenever we made public appearances.

STEVE: Are you suggesting you did not?

THEODORA: *(She gives him a sharp look.)* Perhaps because I had had so *little* comfort and pleasure as a child, I revelled in it as an adult.

STEVE: *(Surprised)* So little pleasure, as a prostitute?

THEODORA: You are naive, sir. Prostitutes pretend to be pleased. They are primarily actresses.

But don't imagine Justinian was simply a creature of vanity. He was a leader who believed in law, and was a Christian who believed in your version of God, Augustine.

STEVE: What were some more of Justinian's accomplishments?

THEODORA: He freed Africa from the Vandals, took Italy back from the Ostrogoths, and recovered a portion of Spain from the Visigoths.

STEVE: Your Majesty, we are told that Justinian's sleep requirements were minimal. Is that true?

THEODORA: Indeed it is.

STEVE: I envy him that. Some described him as the Emperor who never slept.

THEODORA: Nonsense. But he did seem to be adequately refreshed after just an hour or two of sleep.

STEVE: That fascinates me, partly because my normal sleep cycle is eleven hours a night.

THEODORA: Really? You and I have that in common.

STEVE: Is that right? But I envy men like Justinian—Thomas Edison, Chou En-Lai—who needed so little sleep.

RUSSELL: Mr. Allen, you would appear to have been unconscious some 45 percent of your life! *(With a smile)* You might have accomplished a great deal but for that.

STEVE: But on the other hand, your Lordship, one can do no harm while asleep.

Your Majesty, what was the official attitude, during Justinian's reign, to an issue which in recent years, in Western nations, has attracted a great deal of public attention and commentary, that of homosexuality?

THEODORA: In the first year of Justinian's reign the Bishop of Rhodes and the Bishop of Diospholis were found guilty of such unnatural practices. High church authorities dismissed them from their posts. Justinian had them arrested, castrated, and paraded through the streets of Constantinople in disgrace.

AUGUSTINE: He was right to do so! The sins which are against nature, like those of the men of Sodom, are at all times and places to be not only detested, but punished! God's law did not make men so that they should use each other thus.

RUSSELL: Father, your harshness on this question could be defended only if it could be demonstrated that homosexual acts resulted from a decision of will. They do not. No one decides to be a homosexual any more than you decided to be a heterosexual! But there was one other aspect, my friends, *(to audience)* in which conditions in ancient Constantinople were like those of your modern world, and that is that superstition ruled the day.

AUGUSTINE: Yes. Fortunetellers, astrologers, soothsayers, and frauds of all kinds preyed on the ignorance of the people.

THEODORA: Oh, come, come, gentlemen! There was scarcely any society worthy of the name in our time. People must believe in something. So, yes, we did believe in charms, incantations, astrologers, magic potions.

JEFFERSON: In Her Majesty's day there was at least an excuse for such beliefs. There is *no* such excuse in the modern world.

RUSSELL: Yes, it's really depressing to hear people who look perfectly intelligent excusing their bad behavior by saying, "Well, after all, I'm a Taurus," or "Naturally, he drinks a lot; he's a Capricorn." Now, really!

AUGUSTINE: But to return to Her Majesty's time, my friends, there was one happy result from this terrible morass of sin, corruption, ignorance, and despair. In the Egyptian capital of Alexandria, particularly, there was a sudden resurgence of religious faith and practice. The very difficulty of the time increased the numbers of the devout.

THEODORA: Yes, gentlemen. I found myself in Alexandria at this time, having left my lover, Hekebolus. I met some of the holy men, and women, of whom Augustine speaks. The patriarch, Timothy, in particular, became my spiritual father.

STEVE: The drama of the Nika riots had considerable historic importance, coming as they did so early in Justinian's reign. Exactly what was the point of the Nika riots, and why were they identified by the name *Nika*?

THEODORA: We had two rival factions, the Greens and the Blues. Originally they cared only about the Hippodrome games, but in time they became involved in more important matters. For a long time the Emperors had been able to play one faction against the other, but in this new instance the common people were angry about taxation, corruption in government, inflation.

RUSSELL: Yes. Consequently, the Greens and the Blues joined forces in order to—as they would have liked to see it—throw the rascals out, meaning Justinian and Her Majesty.

THEODORA: They shouted the word, "*Nika! Nika!*" which means conquer, or victory. Fires were started about the city. Justinian hurried to the Hippodrome, hoping to quiet the furious mob with a speech. But the people were not convinced by his words, well-chosen as they were.

JEFFERSON: Justinian was tempted to resign on the spot and flee, I understand.

THEODORA: Yes, Mr. President. But I was strong if he was—for the moment—*weak*. I said to him, "If there were left to me no other safety but in flight, I would not fly! Those who have worn the crown should never survive its loss. *Never* will I see the day when I am not hailed as Empress. If you wish to fly, Caesar"—I said to him—"well and good. You have the money, the ships are ready, the sea is clear. But I shall stay, for I love the old proverb that says, 'The royal purple is the best shroud.'" Justinian drew strength from my words and we won the moment!

AUGUSTINE: *(Dryly)* With the help of the army.

THEODORA: Of course. Our defenders had to kill thirty thousand of the rabble to restore order.

JEFFERSON: Mr. Allen, your listeners might grasp the extent of the power wielded by Her Majesty if they are told that she actually dictated—to your church, Augustine—the appointment of a pope!

STEVE: What?!

RUSSELL: Yes. You see, in the year 556 the Vicar of Christ, the Bishop of Rome, was Pope Agapetus. The Pope and Her Majesty strongly— er—disapproved of each other.

STEVE: Why?

THEODORA: Because I was a Monophysite Christian. Agapetus had expelled our holy leader from Constantinople. The Pope was, in fact, attacking Monophysite leaders throughout the Empire. He even had the nerve to attack us in Egypt, where we were the dominant Christian faction!

After Pope Agapetus died his successors continued his policy. However, one prominent Roman Catholic churchman—the Deacon Vigilius—had been wise enough to curry favor with me, and he had promised that if he ever became pope he would adopt a more reasonable policy toward us Monophysites. When Agapetus died I supplied Vigilius with money and hurried him off to Rome. Unfortunately a man named Severus had already been elected.

STEVE: So your plans had been frustrated. How could you possibly do anything about that, once the church had made its decision?

THEODORA: I communicated with Vigilius, and also with my close friend Antonina, who was the wife of the great General Belisarius.

RUSSELL: Another reformed prostitute.

THEODORA: Yes! We agreed to suggest to Balisarius that Pope Severus had plotted to hand over the city of Rome to the Goths.

STEVE: Did General Belisarius believe that?

JEFFERSON: Evidently not, Mr. Allen. The religious side of the dispute was of little importance to him. His concerns were purely political. He suggested to the Pope that the church ought to work out a compromise with the Monophysites. Unfortunately for Severus he refused repeated requests to be so—er—reasonable.

AUGUSTINE: He was absolutely right to refuse! One can not compromise on matters of principle!

THEODORA: *(Contemptuously)* Principle! Hah! Belisarius knew how to deal with such impertinence! He summoned the Pope to his palace and dismissed his personal guard.

RUSSELL: It was the General's wife—your close friend Antonina—who was in charge of things.

THEODORA: That's right! She gave the Pope a sound tongue-lashing, had him thrown in a cell and put aboard a ship to the east! A short week later my man Vigilius was consecrated Pope of your church, Augustine!

AUGUSTINE: After so many centuries, Your Majesty, are you still proud of your infamous maneuvering?

THEODORA: I am proud, sir, of my power!

JEFFERSON: In Her Majesty's defense, Mr. Allen, it must be said that because of her background. . . .

THEODORA: Do not patronize me, sir!

JEFFERSON: And Constantinople, itself, was in her day one of the most corrupt cities known to history.

STEVE: In what way, specifically, Mr. President?

JEFFERSON: In all possible ways, sir. Adultery flourished. Prostitution was openly flaunted. Houses of ill-repute were even established in the shadows of churches and monasteries.

THEODORA: The close proximity of church and bawdy-house sir, was not unique to Constantinople. Have you read the Old Testament?

JEFFERSON: Of course.

THEODORA: Then you must know of the Temple prostitutes repeatedly mentioned in the Scriptures!

JEFFERSON: Vice is vice, Your Majesty, regardless of its point of origin. And every form of it—the natural and the unnatural—flourished in your city. Gambling, too, had the populace in a frenzy.

The Hippodrome, as you've reminded us, was the center of all this corruption. Not only did the two political and social factions dissipate their energies with nonsensical concentration on the outcome of athletic contests, but practically *all* the people were more interested in the games, the races, the executions at the Hippodrome, than they were in important moral, social, or political questions.

THEODORA: Mr. Jefferson, it seems very strange to me that an American would be so critical of the popular entertainment in the old Hippodrome. In your own country at present there are hundreds of similar stadiums where your citizens are roused to a frenzy by athletic competitions, by gambling, by drinking.

I also find it terribly amusing that an American would lecture any other country or its people on the subject of corruption, either sexual or financial! Your own cities are such cesspools of thievery, degeneracy, crime, pornography, and prostitution that there are neighborhoods, I understand, where decent women and children cannot walk down the street!

JEFFERSON: Your point, Your Majesty, is—God help us—all too well taken. I pray that my countrymen may perceive the error of their present ways before it is too late.

THEODORA: *(Derisively)* Oh, too late for what? The common rabble will always want broad entertainment. Only a few are seriously interested in the arts, in the sciences, in philosophy.

JEFFERSON: In your day, Your Majesty, there was some excuse for this in that the common people could neither read nor write. But those of us who founded this nation—Washington, Madison, Adams, Franklin, Paine, Monroe, and the rest—we foresaw the day when an ever-growing number of American citizens would avail themselves of the benefits of education, for it is education that can create a more civilized, a more humane society!

THEODORA: Oh, come off it! Look about your country today, sir! Millions have gone through your universities. Has this produced a vast generation of scholars, of scientists, artists, philosophers? Hardly! Your people are, indeed, for the most part, literate, while mine were not. But what do you Americans read? The works of philosophers? Of historians? Of theologians? Of other scholars? Of your few great poets or novelists? The question is ridiculous.

JEFFERSON: I assure you, Your Majesty, I am as saddened by this as you are contemptuous of it. But I quite agree with what I take to be the implication of your remarks, that a democratic society without effective popular education is meaningless, perhaps even dangerous. If a nation expects to be both ignorant and free, it expects what never was and never will be.

AUGUSTINE: But, Mr. President, error has no rights. There is no natural right to publish harmful falsehoods!

JEFFERSON: My dear friend, both books and newspapers must be written in freedom. If the facts in a book are false, then they should be disproved by those who know the truth. But, for God's sake, let us freely hear both sides!

RUSSELL: Bravo! The war against illiteracy and other ignorance, Augustine, must *not* be conducted in the way in which your church has waged it over the centuries, for the primary purpose of your educators was religious indoctrination! You refused to teach any science except that which could be harmonized with your Scriptures. Since they are utterly unscientific, this meant that your education, in the sciences, was faulty and inferior.

AUGUSTINE: Russell, there were great individual scholars and scientists *within* the church.

RUSSELL: Indeed there were, and when they were alive your church hampered and harassed them. In some cases it even excommunicated and killed them! Perhaps, we cannot blame either the church or our educational institutions alone for the present unhappy state of affairs in which people are perhaps becoming less rather than more intelligent. But I believe that now—for the first time in history—there are technological reasons for hope.

STEVE: And those reasons are—?

RUSSELL: Television, radio, and the rest of the popular media. Consider: Augustine, one of history's greatest instructors, was able to reach only a relatively small audience, even through his writings. But now—at this moment—he is being seen by millions of people. Television has a tremendous potential for education, a potential as yet hardly realized.

THEODORA: Would it be safe to say then, gentlemen, that a glance about the modern world will lead you to be less contemptuous of customs in the Constantinople of my day?

JEFFERSON: Agreed, Your Majesty, but we were speaking not only of popular ignorance and superstition, but of vice and depravity.

THEODORA: See here, sir, don't pose as a secular saint in my presence! You are considered a humanitarian, but you kept *slaves* on your plantation, did you not!?

JEFFERSON: I do not deny it. Yes, I kept slaves. About 150 at one period. Most of the estates in Virginia kept slaves. They constituted the work body and they tended to come with the property. They were born on the estates and lived their lives on them. To have set them "free" at that time would have been irresponsible. Where would these poor people have gone? What would they have done? They would have become public charges. I can only tell you, Your Majesty, that I tried to treat them well. The whip was never used, common though it was in those days, as in your own. I wrote an antislavery clause into the Declaration of Independence, but it was struck by Congress. In 1778, however, I succeeded in having a law passed prohibiting the further importation of slaves. Sad to say, it took many more years and a bloody and bitter civil war before the practice of slavery was abolished. So for me it was a matter of living within a system, and I tried to do that as decently as possible.

THEODORA: You were married, were you?

JEFFERSON: Yes, Your Majesty. I married Martha Wayles Skelton in 1772. It was a good marriage but lasted only ten years, due to her death.

THEODORA: Mr. President, is it true you later had a mistress, and that she was a slave? *(A quiet pause as the other guests look at each other, somewhat uncomfortably. Jefferson takes a breath.)*

JEFFERSON: You are referring to Sally Hemmings. The bluntness of your question makes our relationship seem sordid, which it certainly was not. Since we loved each other for a very long time, and did not marry, yes, the word *mistress* applies, although it's a word with unkind connotations.

Sally was a malatto, or quadroon, partly Negro. Her father was John Wayles, my wife's father, and although they had different mothers, and so were half sisters, they resembled each other closely.

Sally was a child of nine when Martha died.

The relationship that later developed between us was a deeply personal one. She and I did not know each other simply because I was the master of the estate and she was a slave. My wife was dead. Sally Hemmings and I loved each other. I think that is enough explanation.

THEODORA: I can understand such feelings, having felt them myself. But why, if you felt so strongly about the woman, did you never marry her?

JEFFERSON: We had a new nation, Your Majesty, yes, but human nature did not automatically change with it. I was a political figure. An interracial marriage at that time was unacceptable. It would have caused a scandal. No one knew that better than Sally.

Criticize me if you will but I had to make a choice: my importance to my country, or my own gratification. And lest you think my association with Sally Hemmings was frivolous, I tell you that it lasted thirty-eight years and that we had three children.

STEVE: Thank you, Mr. President; and on that note, my friends, we conclude, because we have no more time. Thank you all, and good night.

SHOW # 15

Aristotle
(BERNARD BEHRENS)

Niccolo Machiavelli
(ALFRED RYDER)

Elizabeth Barrett Browning
(JAYNE MEADOWS)

Sun Yat-Sen
(KEYE LUKE)

Welcome to another Meeting of Minds.

Our guests this evening are:

From Greece of the fourth century B.C., the philosopher, Aristotle.

From sixteenth-century Italy, Niccolo Machiavelli.

From nineteenth-century England, poet Elizabeth Barrett Browning.

And from twentieth-century China, Sun Yat-Sen.

And now—your host—Mr. Steve Allen.

STEVE: Good evening and welcome to another Meeting of Minds. Our first guest—Sun Yat-Sen—known as the father of modern China— was a part-time medical doctor who became a full-time revolutionary. Oddly enough he is considered a hero by both the Chinese Communists and their enemies, Chiang Kai-Shek's Nationalists. And the list of leaders popular with both Communists and anti-Communists is a very short list indeed. Welcome, please, Sun Yat-Sen. *(He enters, bows.)* *(Superimpose: Sun Yat-Sen 1866–1925)* Welcome, Dr. Sun. We are very honored.

SUN: Thank you, Mr. Allen.

STEVE: Would you care for some tea?

SUN: Yes, thank you.

STEVE: *(Pouring tea)* We were speculating, just before we came on the air, on the nature of patience, Dr. Sun. It's usually assumed that the Oriental has an advantage in this regard over the Caucasian.

SUN: An advantage? In what way?

STEVE: Well, many people say that the Oriental is by nature and training a patient person—a tentative hypothesis, Dr. Sun, on which I welcome your instruction.

SUN: You have chosen the wrong instructor. When I was a young man, our country was seething with corruption, crippled by poverty, hunger, disease. I could wait for the evil to eat itself out, but I spent my life most impatiently destroying the infection so that a new, healthy system could develop. But your question reminds me of a conversation I had many years ago with some Russians. It was—uh—about 1900 and I was in a library in London doing some studying. The Russians and I happened to strike up a conversation and soon realized that we were revolutionary comrades.

One of the Russians asked me: How long will it take the revolution to succeed? I did not know how to answer. I was then in the exile which followed my first defeat. Since I couldn't be active at home I served the revolution by educating the world about the terrible conditions in China. But I was also depressed, and at times, even discouraged. I carefully considered the question, and gave my most conservative estimate. "Perhaps the revolution will succeed in thirty years."

The Russians were very surprised. "In such an enormous country as yours," they said, "can you succeed in only thirty years?" I thought they were being sarcastic, so I said, "How long will it take for your revolution to succeed?"

They answered: "If we can succeed in one hundred years, we shall be satisfied, but for now we are struggling. If we do not struggle now, we shall not succeed in a hundred years."

Reflecting on what I had told them, I felt very much ashamed.

STEVE: Ashamed? Why?

SUN: Because I knew their success was many times surer, and their undauntable spirit many times greater than my own.

STEVE: If that incident in the London library occurred in 1900, Dr. Sun—then the Russians' hundred years became seventeen . . . and your waiting period of thirty years became only eleven.

SUN: Yes. But if you are committed to change you must work for it. It isn't enough to just feel opposed to pollution or crime or pornography or war. If you want conditions to change you must unite with others and act—do!

STEVE: Dr. Sun, I wonder how a medical doctor becomes a revolutionary. In this country, the AMA wouldn't permit it.

SUN: *(He laughs.)* Actually, my medical training was a step toward the religious ministry. In either case, my profession was simply a means by which I could serve my people.

STEVE: You entered the ministry?

SUN: I considered it. As a teenager, you see, I had been converted to Christianity by foreign missionaries. I am deeply indebted to those good people, Mr. Allen. It was *they* who placed the ideal of freedom in my heart.

STEVE: In what sense were the Chinese in your day not a free people?

SUN: We were shamelessly exploited by foreign powers, and brutalized by tyrants at home. We were chained by centuries of religious superstition, ignorance, by disease, by opium, by prostitution, by slavery.

STEVE: Literally? Slavery of what sort?

SUN: Tradition actually permitted Chinese parents to sell their own sons into bondage, and their daughters into prostitution. But in the larger sense, my people were slaves to a corrupt foreign dynasty which taxed and terrorized to maintain itself in power.

STEVE: A foreign dynasty, you say?

SUN: Yes, the Manchu emperors were invaders from Manchuria. They were Orientals, of course, but not Chinese.

STEVE: Ah, yes. Her Majesty, the Dowager Empress Tz'u Hsi, explained that to us when she was here. But that sort of tyranny had been going on for centuries. Why should a revolution in China be more likely to succeed in the early 1900s than at any time before?

SUN: In addition to the domestic brutality I have described, my people were now subject to new indignities at the hands of shamelessly greedy foreigners. These new exploiters—mostly Europeans—had special privileges in China, under a series of one-sided treaties which robbed my people of their independence.

STEVE: Why didn't the Chinese army throw the Europeans out?

SUN: There was no such thing as the Chinese army, in the Western sense. Our separate military groups had neither the will, nor, I'm afraid, the ability to fight back. And our people were at war with themselves: peasant against landlord, country against city, south against north, son against father, new against old.

STEVE: I don't wish to sound callous, but it seems to me that your people were suffering no more than their ancestors had. Again, was there some special difference that made the revolution more likely to succeed after the turn of the century?

SUN: *(He thinks for a moment.)* Yes. Tradition-bound as our life was, a certain amount of enlightenment had taken place.

STEVE: How?

SUN: Partly as a result of contracts with Europeans.

STEVE: The very people who were, in part, responsible for your enslavement?

SUN: Yes.

STEVE: Fascinating.

SUN: Though I'm quite sure none of the foreigners realized it at the time, they had stowaways among their imports: Western science, Western philosophy, Western political thinking. Gradually we came to realize that our land did not belong to foreign investors, or to the Emperors, the warlords, or the landowners. Some of us came to believe that the earth belongs to all God's people and not just to a powerful few.

STEVE: But it took also the dedication of men like yourself, Dr. Sun, to convert your idealistic, revolutionary theory into action.

SUN: I was but one among many, Mr. Allen. And our spirit was not confined to China. Revolutionary momentum was rising everywhere in Russia, Turkey, and in Mexico at this time.

But, Mr. Allen, I'm most eager to meet your other guests. I feel rather humble in the light of their greatness.

STEVE: Dr. Sun, you are a hero to nine hundred million people, and greatly admired by others as well. I'm sure our other guests will be honored to meet you.

SUN: Thank you.

STEVE: During the sixteenth century in Renaissance Italy there were two books which were considered essential for any ambitious young nobleman. The first was Castiglione's *Book of the Courtier.* The second was *The Prince,* written by our next guest, Niccolo Machiavellli.

Just as yours, Dr. Sun, was a world in revolution, so was Machiavelli's. Gutenberg had just invented the printing press. Columbus in 1492 made the incredible discovery of new, undreamed of continents! Luther was about to unveil his remarkable drama. And the writings of Aristotle, Plato, and other ancient Greeks and Romans had suddenly swept through the European mind. A new artistic explosion occurred. What a time to be alive!

But the separate city-states of Italy were in turmoil.

For three centuries, Machiavelli, the son of a Florentine lawyer, was called a monster, an immoral cynic, and a product of the Devil. Recently, critics have been somewhat more charitable—which gives hope to us all. Ladies and gentlemen, from Renaissance Italy . . . Niccolo Machiavelli. *(Machiavelli enters. He is crisp, humorless, argumentative, but not defensive. There is a bloodlessness to him and a cold absolute belief in everything he says—the more immoral the statement the more icy he becomes.) (Superimpose: Niccolo Machiavelli, 1469–1527)* Welcome, *Signore* Machiavelli. How do you account, sir, for the—

MACHIAVELLI: One moment, Mr. Allen. You've just called me a monster in front of *(indicates television audience)* millions of people.

STEVE: No, sir. I said others have so described you. I apologize if you're offended but that is your reputation, among most people.

MACHIAVELLI: And precisely what was my monstrous immorality? To seek the truth of government, instead of glorifying some unrealistic Utopia. I wrote of real men in real situations.

Dr. Sun, the man who professes perfect goodness in everything cannot survive in a world where so much is not good. And if this man is a leader, a father to the people—*(Makes a gesture of helplessness.)*

SUN: I find your disregard for political ideals very—er—

MACHIAVELLI: Infuriating?

SUN: No, I would say depressing. You certainly departed from former writings on the subject, such as those of Aristotle.

MACHIAVELLI: Ah, Dr. Sun, I described what *is* and not what ought to be. If you had taken my advice, perhaps you would not have failed as first president of the Chinese Republic. You, sir, are a perfect example of how not to preside over a government! My book—

STEVE: *(Picks up book.) The Prince.*

MACHIAVELLI: *Il Principa.* It shows how to acquire, retain, and expand power, in a real world of men. Not an imaginary textbook world. Or a world of—*como ce dici*—Sunday-school ideals.

SUN: Nevertheless you are not short of critics, *Signore* Machiavelli. Churchmen, philosophers, historians, and statesmen through the centuries have—I understand—condemned your view of the so-called real world of men.

STEVE: That's right! Frederick the Great, for example, said that you corrupted politics and attempted to destroy the very precepts of sound morality!

MACHIAVELLI: Ah, Frederick. The despot horrified by despotism.

STEVE: You take exception to his remarks?

MACHIAVELLI: *(With a smile)* It is entirely possible that Frederico may have been following my advice.

STEVE: What advice was that?

MACHIAVELLI: That the prince must always seem to be virtuous and uncorrupted! Of course, one way to do this is to condemn something which is generally held to be corrupt. Many of your political people *today* do this sort of thing. You see, men observe only what the prince appears to be. Few know what he is. *(To Steve)* Have not you Americans learned that, in recent times?

SUN: My friend, you too quickly dismiss the importance of virtue in politics. I agree that part of human nature is base. But—the prince, someone who is to lead, surely he cannot be equally unvirtuous. He must be superior—preeminent in virtue, to serve as an inspiration! As a wise father teaches and inspires his children, for example. Aristotle went so far as to say that when such a man is identified, he should be king for life.

MACHIAVELLI: *(A beat)* Very touching. But where does such a man actually exist? Moral virtue in a political leader can neither preserve the state nor the power of the prince who rules it!

SUN: *(Shaking his head)* We do no harm if we set our sights high, my friend.

STEVE: Your ideal prince sounds more like a beast than a human.

MACHIAVELLI: You are quite right, sir. The prince must know the way of the beast as well as the man. He must imitate the fox and the lion. One must be a fox to recognize traps and a lion to frighten wolves. Many good men, sincere men, have only played the noble lion, pretending disinterest in the baser nature of man. And where are they now? Deposed, assassinated, exiled. Where now are their kingdoms? Their virtuous laws?

SUN: I grant that the best is often unattainable, but this is all the more reason for the statesman to at least be acquainted with the best possible behavior in particular circumstances. But most importantly, he should know the best as ideal—to use as both guide and goal.

MACHIAVELLI: To be trustworthy, generous, humane, religious, and honest?

SUN: Of course. One cannot be a good ruler who does not exercise such qualities.

MACHIAVELLI: Must he also be ready at all times to exercise the opposite of these qualities?

SUN: Yes . . . but under very limited circumstances.

MACHIAVELLI: Such circumstances are the only ones we see in the world! Even as Aristotle has written: "Let his disposition be virtuous, or at least half-virtuous; and if he must be wicked, let him be half-wicked only."

SUN: You seem to miss the point that—

MACHIAVELLI: Neither of us shall miss the point, Dr. Sun, if we remember that the imagination of utopians has created many principalities and republics that have never actually been seen or known. Sir Thomas More, I understand, visited you earlier, Mr. Allen?

STEVE: Yes.

MACHIAVELLI: He brilliantly described his Utopia. But he never created it. Karl Marx, besides criticizing the evils of capitalism . . . sketched out a design for a socialist paradise. I simply describe techniques which assure the survival of the prince and consequently of the state.

STEVE: You know, one of the sad aspects of this debate, gentlemen, is that it is an argument between two Christians.

MACHIAVELLI: This is unusual? We Christians have been arguing for two-thousand years!

SUN: Yes, unfortunately.

MACHIAVELLI: But let us not be confused on this point. Politics is an activity that has no place for Christian morality.

STEVE: No place?

MACHIAVELLI: No place at all! Look what happened to the old pagan Roman Empire when it succumbed to Christian ideas. It collapsed.

SUN: Machiavelli, it is not necessary for me to refute you. There is no pope of your church—no theologian—who agrees with you on this! Your entire Western civilization is founded upon Christian morality. And this you repudiate. With such friends as you the Christian church does not need enemies!

STEVE: Well. Not many of her admirers are aware that our next guest took an interest in the politics of Italy, in her own day. Elizabeth Barrett Browning, who lived a century ago, was a gifted poet. Her courage, intelligence, and social consciousness and passion are all expressed in her work. But the fascinating story of her personal life has—in a sense—somewhat overshadowed her poetry.

Her marriage to Robert Browning became one of history's most romantic love stories, concerning which countless books, plays, and film-scripts have been written. Welcome, please . . . Elizabeth Barrett Browning.

ELIZABETH: *(She enters, descending staircase, leading a brown spaniel.)* *(Superimpose: Elizabeth Barrett Browning, 1806–1861)* No, Flush. You can't stay with me just now. You must wait. But just come along and say hello to the nice gentlemen. Mr. Allen, Flush didn't want to stay upstairs without me. I wonder, could he—Oh, look, Flush. Macaroons! Could I have a macaroon, please? Yes, you'll get one, darling. Thank you. There now, you run along and be a good boy. *(She sits.)* We've been together so many, many years. . . . One does get deeply attached. It's my fault. I spoiled him terribly.

STEVE: Would you care for some tea, Mrs. Browning?

ELIZABETH: Yes, thank you.

SUN: May I? *(He pours.)*

STEVE: Thank you, Dr. Sun.

MACHIAVELLI: Niccolo Machiavelli. I am delighted to meet you, *Signora* Browning.

ELIZABETH: *È mio piacere, Signore.*

MACHIAVELLI: *Mille graci.*

STEVE: Mrs. Browning, I must tell you that one of my most cherished books is a volume of your poems.

ELIZABETH: How kind. I do hope you have a copy of Robert's.

STEVE: Oh, yes. *(He looks about the table.)* Well. I imagine it must be very exciting for three such interesting people to meet each other. *(The men smile and nod.)*

SUN: Indeed.

MACHIAVELLI: *Si.*

ELIZABETH: Oh, it is. I find the idea very stimulating . . . almost too stimulating.

STEVE: Oh? Why is that?

ELIZABETH: Until I met Robert excitement was difficult for me to deal with. For most of my life I lived as an invalid.

SUN: Really?

ELIZABETH: Yes, Dr. Sun, in one room. A very quiet life, I assure you.

STEVE: But how could you have quiet in your house with nine brothers and sisters?

ELIZABETH: Ten.

STEVE: *Ten* brothers and sisters. Your mother must have had her hands full.

ELIZABETH: Oh, no. We were cared for by nursemaids and governesses on our estate at Hope End. That is, before we lost our money. My mother was such a sweet, quiet soul she never could have raised eleven children alone.

STEVE: Your father, I understand, was one of those gentlemen who was decidedly the master of his own home.

ELIZABETH: Yes, that's true, Mr. Allen. My mother would never have dreamt of challenging his authority. I was Papa's favorite and whenever Mother wanted something she came to *me* and I would ask him for it, in her behalf. I did the same for my brothers and sisters.

MACHIAVELLI: That doesn't sound as if your parents were very close.

ELIZABETH: Perhaps not in the way you would understand it. But, after my mother's death, my father would not allow a single thing of hers to be moved. Everything was kept just exactly as she had left it.

STEVE: Your father never remarried?

ELIZABETH: *(She shakes her head.)* No.

STEVE: Our knowledge of your father is primarily confined to novels and plays. Is it true that after your mother died he never grieved openly for her?

ELIZABETH: Yes, it is true. He never shed a single tear, and we children were forbidden to cry.

STEVE: How tragic, to lose your mother when you were just a child and not be able . . . how old were you when she died?

ELIZABETH: I was twenty-two. And I'd been an invalid for seven years.

SUN: Because of my medical training, Mrs. Browning, I find myself curious about the cause of your illness.

ELIZABETH: When I was fifteen, Dr. Sun, I had fallen from my pony, while riding against my father's wishes! I disobeyed my father and I was punished. I felt God had afflicted me.

SUN: The Creator of the universe, my dear, does not act in so petty and spiteful a way.

MACHIAVELLI: Mrs. Browning, it's interesting to me that many famous writers found the time for their labors because they were confined to bed. Was it during this period that you began to create your exquisite poetry?

ELIZABETH: No, sir. They tell me I was hardly out of the cradle when I began to make up verses. Words were magic to me. I learned to read at three, and as long as I can remember books and dreams were what I lived in.

STEVE: How old were you when you wrote your first poem?

ELIZABETH: Six. Papa was so pleased he named me the Poet Laureate of our house! When one of my poems was especially good he rewarded me with money.

SUN: Strange.

ELIZABETH: This greatly encouraged me.

STEVE: I understand your father had a superb library! I imagine you must have read almost everything in it.

ELIZABETH: Unfortunately, no. Papa warned me, "Ba, you may read the books on this side but not on that side." Because the—

MACHIAVELLI: Excuse. Ba?

ELIZABETH: *(aside to Machiavelli)* Yes, Ba. Oh, that was what the family called me.—Because on that side of the room, you see, were the forbidden books.

SUN: Forbidden? What books were you forbidden to read?

ELIZABETH: Oh, *Tom Jones,* Gibbon's history of Rome. But I didn't mind, really. There were so many wonderful books on my side.

MACHIAVELLI: Such as?

ELIZABETH: The Bible, Shakespeare, Milton, Plato, Aristotle. What an honor it will be to meet him.

STEVE: Indeed. You read Milton, Plato, Aristotle. Most young children today wouldn't even know their names, much less read them.

ELIZABETH: A great pity. I also read Thomas Paine's *Age of Reason,*
Voltaire's *Philosophical Dictionary,* and the essays of—

STEVE: Your father permitted you to read those?

ELIZABETH: *(She laughs nervously.)* Oh dear, no. He had so many books,
Mr. Allen, he couldn't keep track of them all. Voltaire made such
a powerful impression on me that after reading him I prayed, "Oh,
God, if there be a God, save my soul. If I have a soul."

Oh, could we meet Aristotle now?

STEVE: Certainly. It's remarkable how many of the illustrious personages from history who have appeared here have mentioned Aristotle.
Sometimes in admiration, sometimes in relative disparagement. But
the very fact that his name has come up, repeatedly, and in connection with so many areas of scholarship—demonstrates his profound
importance in the history of not just Western but human thought.
For hundreds of years his eminence was such that he was referred
to as simply "The Philosopher."

SUN: I understand that Dante Alighieri referred to Aristotle as the
"master of those who know." And that Charles Darwin acknowledged his personal debt to Aristotle.

STEVE: Yes. Those of our earlier guests, such as Galileo and Sir Francis
Bacon, who have referred to Aristotle in some annoyance, were
actually not so much criticizing him as the misuse of his authority by the church. Aristotle's achievements, in other words, were
so impressive, so great, that it finally became unthinkable—even
in some cases dangerous—to question his authority. In any event,
here is—Aristotle! *(Aristotle enters.) (Superimpose: Aristotle 384–
322 B.C.)* Welcome, sir. It's a great honor to meet you.

ARISTOTLE: *(He remains standing.)* Thank you, sir. But the experience
is even more dramatic for me.

STEVE: Oh? In what way?

ARISTOTLE: Well, you are meeting only one of me. But I am meeting
hundreds of you. *(He indicates all present.)* And am, I understand,
addressing millions more.

STEVE: I hadn't thought of that.

ARISTOTLE: *(With a smile)* Think of it.

STEVE: I shall.

ARISTOTLE: And I am as astounded by the appearance of your modern world *(he looks about)* as you would be if you returned to
earth twenty-four hundred years into the future. But I was appalled,
sir, to hear you say that my writings have been used to retard

the exploration of knowledge. I don't think that anyone who creates new ideas ever considers his work the last word on the subject.

STEVE: Ah. Well, make yourself comfortable, sir. *(Steve and Aristotle sit.)*

ARISTOTLE: *(Nodding)* Mrs. Browning. Gentlemen.

STEVE: Before we get to the details of your philosophy, sir, I'd like to ask a few basic questions about your life.

ARISTOTLE: Do you mean to say that its details are not known in your country?

STEVE: I'm afraid they're not very well known, sir. We do know that you lived in Athens in the so-called Golden Age of Greece, and I—

ARISTOTLE: *(He gives him a look.)* Do you, in fact, actually know that?

SUN: *(He laughs.)* Ah, I see we're starting with the philosophy after all.

STEVE: No, in the strict sense of the verb *to know,* I do not personally know of the truth of what I just said.

ARISTOTLE: I'm glad to hear you say that because you cannot possibly know anything that is not, in fact, the case. And—as it happens—I did not live in Athens during that city's Golden Age. The Greek city-state system was already in decline when I was born.

STEVE: And that would be 384 years before Christ.

ARISTOTLE: Yes. In the Macedonian town of Stagira.

STEVE: I see. Was your father a philosopher?

ARISTOTLE: No, he was a doctor—personal physician and friend to King Amyntas II of Macedonia. While you might be unfamiliar with Amyntas, I assume you Americans have heard of his son, Philip II of Macedonia.

STEVE: Oh, yes.

ARISTOTLE: Well, Philip considerably increased the power of the kingdom of Macedonia. But in time his son, and my pupil, Alexander, made a far greater name for himself as a conqueror.

STEVE: Indeed, he did. He enlarged the Macedonian empire to encompass a vast area stretching from Greece to the Indian Ocean.

MACHIAVELLI: A glorious achievement.

ARISTOTLE: It did not seem so to the Greeks and other subject tribes.

SUN: You mentioned, sir, that your father was a doctor. Was there anything unusual about his choosing medicine as a career?

ARISTOTLE: Not at all, Dr. Sun. Our family was of noble origin and there had been a number of physicians in our line of descent. It was believed, in fact, that we were descended from Asklepios.

STEVE: Asklepios?

ARISTOTLE: He was part god, part physician, and was said to have been the son of the god Apollo and a human princess.

MACHIAVELLI: If you don't mind my asking, Aristotle, did you personally believe that about your ancestor?

ARISTOTLE: *(Smiles, looks about)* Now that it is safe to say such things publicly . . . no, I did not.

In any event, as a boy I was able to benefit from my father's medical training for I assisted him in his practice. Both my parents died, however, while I was still quite young.

STEVE: Who became your guardian thereafter?

ARISTOTLE: A Macedonian official named Proxenus. I also enjoyed the protection of the Macedonian court because of my father's good friendship with King Amyntas. This protection and support continued through the reign of Alexander. But I was ambivalent about the situation.

ELIZABETH: Why?

ARISTOTLE: I was Thracian by birth, Greek by education, and Macedonian by association. But I deplored the Macedonian conquest of Greece. I realized, however, that as the Macedonian empire itself expanded, the area touched by my teachings expanded with it. I passed these war years torn between rejoicing and grieving. I could never forget that I had been Alexander's father in education.

STEVE: You know, when Plato was kind enough to visit us here, he told us that while he had been taught by Socrates, he—Plato— was your instructor.

ARISTOTLE: Indeed, he was. I was eighteen when I began my studies at that great man's academy. You can't imagine how stimulating it was to study with someone who had studied with the immortal Socrates!

SUN: You were eighteen, you say.

ARISTOTLE: Yes, but there were men of all ages at the Academy. Many famous thinkers visited the school.

STEVE: For example.

ARISTOTLE: Theatus, for one *(Sees blank look on Steve's face)*—the father of *solid geometry!* The great astronomer Eudoxus travelled all the way from his home in Asia Minor. All these men had a profound influence on me. And although I would later differ with them as regards one specific or another, I will always be enormously in their debt.

SUN: This, of course, is true of all of us. *(To Steve)* None of your much-heralded scientific or social achievements of the present century could have been accomplished at all if it had not been for the combined efforts of thousands of thinkers, scientists, artists, saints, and seers who lived before you.

ARISTOTLE: You're quite right, Dr. Sun, and some of those early scholars and inventors were Chinese. *(Sun beams and nods a thank you.)* I'm very pleased, sir, that you are convening these Meetings of Minds, as you call them, Mr. Allen, so that at least a few of your illustrious forebears might get a bit of the credit they deserve.

STEVE: Well, gentlemen, we hope over the years to present more than a few of them.

MACHIAVELLI: *Marveouso!*

STEVE: I suppose the lectures in Plato's academy must have been—

ARISTOTLE: May I correct, you, sir?

STEVE: I'm constantly hoping somebody will.

ARISTOTLE: *(Smiling)* I'll be glad to oblige. But there wasn't all that much lecturing, by either Plato or the other teachers at the academy. Plato's method of teaching involved chiefly discussion. It was his intention to follow Socrates' advice in this way. We would consider a particular philosophical problem and then discuss it. Heatedly, enthusiastically.

As a result of this dialectic method—it one day dawned on me that there was a real difference between the kind of knowledge that can be gained through discussion, and another kind acquired by observation and deduction. I also, in time, developed a passion for orderly thinking and discourse.

SUN: Ah, yes. So much of human conversation, you know, is chaotic, disorganized, disorderly. It's no wonder that we humans make so many mistakes. The really remarkable thing perhaps is that we get anything right at all, when we think in such a haphazard fashion.

ARISTOTLE: *(He laughs.)* But I became aware that it was possible to think much more clearly, and I began to develop a system, a set of rules, or guidelines for doing so.

STEVE: Can you be more specific?

ARISTOTLE: I always was. Now all of us become involved in arguments. Sometimes about important matters, sometimes about trivial things. But very few of these arguments are ever resolved to the satisfaction of all parties concerned. And one of the reasons for this is that there is no agreement—among the arguers—about the definition of terms.

STEVE: Terms?

ARISTOTLE: Yes. You might debate the question as to whether a given individual is intelligent. Or artistic. Or courageous. But unless the two arguers agree on the meaning of the terms *intelligent, artistic,* or *courageous,* it will be impossible for them either to come to any agreement or even to understand precisely how they disagree.

STEVE: That all sounds very exciting. But do you think that perhaps because the instructors and students at the academy limited themselves only to the field of philosophy that they might have been—

ARISTOTLE: *(With some humor)* Sir, I am beginning to feel somewhat uncomfortable about having to correct so many of your statements. You seem rather given to the habit of making unwarranted assumptions.

STEVE: Feel free, Aristotle. One of my functions here—I think—is to serve as a horrible example.

ARISTOTLE: *(He and the others laugh heartily.)* Well, I assume that you were using the word *philosophy* in its modern sense—

STEVE: Yes, I was.

ARISTOTLE: Then I wanted to make the correction that the word had a much wider application in my day. Philosophy covered—well— everything. The word *philosophy* simply means love of wisdom, and it is, of course, possible to be wise—or unwise—about any subject at all. We students examined every area of scholarship— science, mathematics, natural history, not just metaphysical or ethical questions.

STEVE: How long did you remain at the academy?

ARISTOTLE: About twenty years. Toward the end of that time I was no longer just a student but was doing some teaching and writing myself.

After Plato died I left Athens.

STEVE: Oh, why?

ARISTOTLE: Greece was suffering through another period of intense warfare among the city-states. Athens itself was, to a very great extent, democratic. I—on the other hand—was known to be closely connected with the Macedonian royal court.

SUN: And it was therefore assumed that your social biases were not favorable to democracy?

ARISTOTLE: The democratic system wasn't working!

MACHIAVELLI: Ah!

ARISTOTLE: The separate factions, the cities, were so involved in internal conflicts that by the time Alexander invaded, the cities were ripe for the taking.

STEVE: So you left Athens to escape the inevitable invasion.

ARISTOTLE: I loved Athens and would gladly have stayed there, invasion or not. But my sympathies were well known; I left town because I cared for my safety. Socrates had died of poison there years earlier. I decided *not* to let Athens sin a second time against philosophy.

MACHIAVELLI: One of your weaknesses as a political philosopher, *amico,* was that you did not perceive that Phillip and Alexander, by their conquests, had forever changed the world. Greece could never return to a system of small independent city-states that you thought were the ideal political form.

ARISTOTLE: It is easy to criticize, my friend, when one has the benefit of hindsight. But some two-thousand years later—in Italy—your society, too, was composed of separate city-states: Florence, Rome, Venice, Pisa—*(Machiavelli mumbles in Italian.)*

STEVE: *(Breaks up fight by interrupting.)* Speaking of that society, Machiavelli, I'd like to know something of the origin, the background, of your best-known book *The Prince.* Your ideal ruler was modeled after Cesare Borgia, is that right?

MACHIAVELLI: Yes.

STEVE: Then why did you dedicate the book to Lorenzo de Medici, the nephew of Pope Leo X?

MACHIAVELLI: *(He smiles.)* It's quite simple. The Medici were then in power. Borgia was not.

STEVE: I see. You had served in the government of Florence?

MACHIAVELLI: *(Proudly)* Yes. As Chancellor of the Second Chancery, and in the Council of Ten of Liberty and Peace.

STEVE: And you continued in this position under the Medici?

MACHIAVELLI: No. They jailed and tortured me, then released me, and exiled me to my ancestral home in the country. It was there that I began work on *The Prince* and many other writings. *The Prince* was written to help the Medici learn in a very short time all that I had learned over many years, and through many hardships and dangers.

STEVE: A sort of "survival handbook" for the prince then in power.

MACHIAVELLI: Yes. But the truth, Mr. Allen, is that I was looking for work. The Medici were my potential employers. My writing showed why it was necessary for a prince to learn how not to be good if he wished to survive. I hoped the gift of this book would earn me a suitable position in the new government. A prince can trust

St. Augustine and Bertrand Russell

All photographs by Mitzi Trumbo

Thomas Jefferson, Empress Theodora, and Steve Allen

Sun Yat-Sen and Steve Allen

Steve Allen, Sun Yat-Sen, Niccolo Machiavelli, and Aristotle

Elizabeth Barrett Browning and Flush

The Dark Lady of the Sonnets, Steve Allen, and William Shakespeare

Othello and Iago

Hamlet, Othello, the Dark Lady, and Romeo

people like myself who will serve more faithfully, to overcome our former errors.

ELIZABETH: Well, sir, I'm glad that by the time Robert and I lived in Italy the Italian revolutionaries were men with much more edifying moral standards than those you professed!

MACHIAVELLI: I always worry when I hear of impractical romantics like yourself taking an interest in politics, *signora.* But, Mrs. Browning, dear lady, I was interested to hear you mention the wonderful library available to you in your childhood. What schools did you attend when—

ELIZABETH: None, sir. Bro and I were tutored because—

STEVE: Bro?

ELIZABETH: Yes, my brother, Edward. My father insisted that our education be purely classical. I spoke Latin and Greek. But Papa refused to let me study mathematics.

SUN: How strange. Why?

ELIZABETH: I have no idea, Dr. Sun. All my life other people handled my finances, and Oh! how I envied anyone who could multiply 3 times 6 without doing it on his fingers! But my love of the Greek language, Aristotle, opened a wonderland of learning to me. I was inspired by the literature of your culture.

ARISTOTLE: Indeed.

ELIZABETH: In fact, I developed such a passionate interest in the ancient Olympian Divinities that I confess I offered secret sacrifices to them.

ARISTOTLE: *(He laughs heartily.)* Really?

ELIZABETH: Yes.

ARISTOTLE: Since you spoke our language and enjoyed our literature did you ever translate any of our writings?

ELIZABETH: Did I! At sixteen I began to translate Aeschylus' *Prometheus Bound.*

ARISTOTLE: Fascinating! And your translation was published?

ELIZABETH: Indeed it was, and the experience was a nightmare.

STEVE: Why?

ELIZABETH: For years the unsold copies were stacked, like a hidden skeleton, in Papa's closet.

STEVE: How sad.

ELIZABETH: Yes. I was enormously depressed by the book's failure. My health suffered. My lungs, you see, had never been very strong.

SUN: You suffered from tuberculosis, did you?

ELIZABETH: I believe so, Dr. Sun. My cough worsened. I brought up

blood. I was really greatly weakened, and became increasingly de-
pendent on my medicine—my elixir.

STEVE: You were confined to bed?

ELIZABETH: No, I spent most of the time lying on the sofa with my
dear faithful dog Flush at my feet. The windows were kept closed
at the doctor's orders, and Papa insisted that the blinds be drawn
down. A pale light filtered through a curtain of vines that grew
outside the window.

STEVE: It sounds like a dreadfully lonely life.

ELIZABETH: Sometimes it was. But Papa was often with me. He was
devoted to me. He would kneel by my side, stroke my hair; he
used to call me his "little Puss," and he'd read to me, by the hour.
He brought me books, gifts. And of course, always the medicines
I needed.

SUN: Medicines for your lungs?

ELIZABETH: Some of them were. But whenever I became excited my
pulse fluttered, and I had great difficulty sleeping. My elixir helped
very much.

STEVE: What were you taking?

ELIZABETH: *(Calmly)* Opium.

SUN: Did your father know that your medicines contained opium?

ELIZABETH: Of course.

STEVE: Opium derivatives still have their legitimate medical use, but
today we recognize that opium is a powerful and dangerous nar-
cotic. In fact, today it is illegal.

ELIZABETH: In my day, sir, the drug was widely used, even in children's
medicines. No one thought it was harmful.

MACHIAVELLI: It is quite unfair to make moral judgments of one age
by the standards of a later time and place.

SUN: Mrs. Browning, you can't be held responsible for what your doctors prescribed. But in my country we fought a war to rid ourselves of this accursed opium!

STEVE: It's a serious enough problem for the United States at the present day, Dr. Sun. Of course, now the traffic in such drugs is largely
in the hands of criminals who—

SUN: A century ago in China the traffic was in the hands of criminals, too. Some of these criminals were highly positioned in the
British government!

ELIZABETH: Dr. Sun, I know nothing of that! My father and my doctors were certainly not criminals.

SUN: Of course not. But it was official British policy to make as much money as possible out of the sale of opium to China! And as if that were not a vicious enough evil . . . the Chinese were forced to pay with silver for the privilege of poisoning themselves. Not only did my people become addicted to this evil drug, but they became even more impoverished by its exorbitant price.

ELIZABETH: Yes, it was costly in England as well. In fact, opium was almost my most expensive item. Papa insisted that I pay for it out of my own income.

SUN: Needless to say, Mrs. Browning, I quite understand that in your country at that same time the average citizen was not aware that opium could be abused.

STEVE: It's a very complex question. Here in our own country—and not terribly many years ago—some of our commercial medicines were largely alcohol, and a good many of them contained opium. The so-called soothing syrups which were given to babies in the U.S. contained the drug. Our cola drinks originally contained small amounts of derivatives of the coca leaf, from which the drug cocaine is made. I think many Americans today don't quite understand why the shops where medicines are purchased were originally called "drug" stores.

ELIZABETH: But Mr. Allen, my opium quieted my pulse and allowed me to sleep.

STEVE: How did you become addicted?

ELIZABETH: I depended on it. But I certainly did not take it for mere amusement. I could not have lived without it, without my red hood of poppies.

STEVE: Did your illness—and, uh—medicine prevent you from writing?

ELIZABETH: No. I soon published a volume called *Seraphim And Other Poems*.

STEVE: Was it a success?

ELIZABETH: *(She shakes her head.)* No, unfortunately it was a dismal failure.

STEVE: Well, were you discouraged at the time by the failure of your second book?

ELIZABETH: Yes, I must admit, I was, and the anxiety weakened me. My pulse rate became so alarming that my doctors insisted I recuperate in a warmer climate. The seacoast town of Torquay. But Papa would not hear of it and he forbad me to take Bro with me.

STEVE: Even though the doctor ordered the trip for your health?

ARISTOTLE: *(He sees the situation.)* Mrs. Browning, your father's love seems very—unnatural.

ELIZABETH: He wanted me—to be near him. I was dangerously ill. He nursed me and carried me about. He cared for me. Finally when the doctors convinced him that my very *life* depended on this trip, he agreed to let me go to Torquay. He even changed his mind and allowed Bro to come with me. I loved Bro more than anything in the world and Papa knew it.

At Torquay my brother held my hand as he had so often, he was so tender, no harsh words, no unkind looks. He held my hand and promised never to leave until I was well. But he did.

STEVE: What happened?

ELIZABETH: We had a silly quarrel, and that afternoon he went on a boating party. There was a sudden squall; the boat capsized. Bro was drowned.

SUN: Were you well enough to go home?

ELIZABETH: No, my health forced me to stay in Torquay alone. For the next fifteen months I heard the ocean waves pounding out the accusation, "You killed him, you killed him, you killed him."

MACHIAVELLI: But, Mrs. Browning, you were not responsible.

ELIZABETH: I was wicked. Papa had warned me! He had not wanted Bro to go to Torquay.

MACHIAVELLI: How old was your brother when he drowned?

ELIZABETH: Thirty-two.

STEVE: Is it true that after you returned from Torquay you remained in your Wimpole Street room for the next five years?

ELIZABETH: *(She nods.)* In one stroke my youth had ended.

STEVE: You know, Mrs. Browning, I think the fact that you suffered as much as you did—even the fact that the two early books you mentioned were unsuccessful—might possibly be more encouraging to many of our viewers than news of your successes.

ARISTOTLE: Ah, indeed.

STEVE: You see, most of us have the impression—about all of the distinguished personages of history who have visited us here—that your lives consisted chiefly of one triumph after another.

MACHIAVELLI: Really? Is the present ignorance really so pronounced?

STEVE: I'm afraid so. But on this point I think it is understandable. It's the final verdict of history—on a great statesman, a poet, an artist, a philosopher—that people tend to remember.

ARISTOTLE: Then it's important indeed that your viewers understand that even the most illustrious personages of history have had at least their share of suffering, struggle, discouragement, unpopularity, and persecution.

MACHIAVELLI: Sometimes even execution.

STEVE: Well . . . you had started to tell us of your life at Wimpole Street during those lonely five years in your room.

SUN: Yes. Seeing hardly any faces must have been very depressing for you.

ELIZABETH: You are mistaken, sir. I had the companionship of my books, and on the walls of my room I could see the dear faces of Wordsworth, Tennyson, Carlyle, Landor, Robert Browning—

STEVE: *(To the others)* Pictures. Mrs. Browning, we mean visitors, friends; people who—

ELIZABETH: *(She is uncomfortable answering.)* Oh well, we were allowed to have people call at certain times, so I did have a few friends. However, Papa refused to meet them—I don't know why—and, of course, no one was ever permitted to dine with us. Papa isolated all of us from the rest of the world.

STEVE: Strange. But how, if you were so completely secluded, how did you meet Robert Browning?

ELIZABETH: I didn't.

STEVE: Yet you managed to get together somehow.

ELIZABETH: Yes, but through letters at first, Mr. Allen. That was how our loving friendship began, and that is how it continued. For five months we wrote to each other, but I would not see him. And yet his first letter to me should have told me how it would end.

MACHIAVELLI: What did he write to you in that first letter?

ELIZABETH: "I love your verses with all my heart, dear Miss Barrett, and I love you, too!"

MACHIAVELLI: In his first letter?

ELIZABETH: Yes. He was writing to me about a volume of my poetry; it had been published in 1844. I had paid tribute in one of the poems to the greatness of Robert Browning. After this we started to correspond regularly. But when he asked permission to visit me I was panic stricken.

STEVE: You mean because of your father?

ELIZABETH: Oh, that was part of it, certainly. But Mr. Browning was a brilliant man. There were few young women in the world who had not seen more, heard more, known more of society than I, who was scarcely young then. What could I possibly offer this passionate, vital young man? It was wonderful enough that such a man would write to me. And then to hear his open profession

of love was—well—I find it impossible to express what it meant
to me.

STEVE: How old was Mr. Browning?

ELIZABETH: Thirty-two.

ARISTOTLE: The same age as Bro. . . .

MACHIAVELLI: And you, if you don't mind my asking?

ELIZABETH: I was thirty-nine. And did not think I had much longer
to live. Robert was young, vigorous, and in the prime of his life.

    Also I did not wish him to be disgraced if he came to our home.

STEVE: Disgraced? What do you mean?

ELIZABETH: A young officer had visited my sister Addles one day when—

MACHIAVELLI: Addles? Pardon me, Mrs. Browning, did all your brothers and sisters have such—er—unusual names?

ELIZABETH: Yes. They were our nursery names. Papa called us by them
all our lives.

    Anyway, the young officer was in our home. My Papa returned
unexpectedly and physically threw him out!

MACHIAVELLI: But what had the young man done?

ELIZABETH: Absolutely nothing. Papa, you see, was determined that
none of us should marry.

MACHIAVELLI: Why not?

ARISTOTLE: Perhaps after his wife's death, Mr. Barrett felt himself
married to you. *(Elizabeth does not speak.)*

STEVE: Well, when was Mr. Browning permitted to come to your home?

ELIZABETH: Tuesday, May 20, 1845, Mr. Allen. I had written to Robert that the visit had to be before 6:00, since that was when Papa
returned home.

STEVE: When did Mr. Browning arrive?

ELIZABETH: On the dot of 3 o'clock. He left at 4:30.

STEVE: Do you remember what you thought when you met Mr.
Browning for the first time?

ELIZABETH: Once I saw him, he never left my mind. I couldn't sleep
that night, even with an extra dose of elixir! It was as if a dream—
or poem—had suddenly come to life! Only Robert, with his joy
in life, his unshakable faith in our future together, and—oh that
energy—only he could have saved me. He found me ill and lonely,
and he cured me. I had felt the shadow of death upon me and
had been brought back to life.

    Then love me, Love! Look on me—
    Breathe on me! As brighter ladies
    do not count it strange, for Love

to give up acres and degree, I
yield the grave for thy sake and
exchange my near sweet view of
Heaven, for earth with thee.

MACHIAVELLI: Bravo!

SUN: How beautiful.

STEVE: It was obviously with his help and his love that you made such progress with your recovery!

ELIZABETH: Yes, yes! One of my dear friends said to me one day, "You are not improved. You are transformed." I took carriage rides, I walked outside in the sun! I, who couldn't walk to my window without help! Even the doctors were amazed. They said that at last, I had the chance for a full recovery! They warned, however, that the foul London weather was deadly, and that I must absolutely winter in Italy or I would undo all the progress I had made. When they spoke of recovery I was elated!

MACHIAVELLI: Did you enjoy Italy?

ELIZABETH: For the first time in twenty-five years I could look forward to a normal life. But Papa said, "There will not be any vacation trips, anywhere." He silenced any discussion! He avoided my room for weeks. That was the way he punished me.

SUN: It sounds as if your father didn't want you to get well!

STEVE: In any event, Mrs. Browning, we know that you did escape from your father and marry Robert Browning. How did that come about?

ELIZABETH: Papa unexpectedly announced that the house was to be redecorated; and that we were all to move immediately to the country. That meant another winter in England. And I knew I could not survive it. His indifference to my health wounded me terribly, but it gave me the right—the duty—to take my life into my own hands.

On September 12th, at Marylebone Church, Robert Browning and I were secretly married. One week later, while Papa was away, taking with me Wilson, my maid, and my darling dog Flush, I slipped out of the house, joined Robert—and we set sail for Italy.

SUN: What did your father do?

ELIZABETH: "My daughter is now in her grave," he said. "Let us forget the dead."

STEVE: God. But in Italy, you and Browning did some of your most productive work, I understand.

ELIZABETH: And reproductive! Our beautiful son, Penini, was born.

STEVE: How old were you at the time?

ELIZABETH: I was forty-three. If anyone had told me, when I was lying as a prisoner in my room on Wimpole Street, that I would one day be married to the man I adored, and bear him a fine and healthy son, I would not, I could not have believed it. But with Robert miracles seemed to happen all the time!

I remember one morning—after breakfast while Robert was looking out the window, I stole up behind him and slipped into his pocket forty-four poems I had written during our courtship and early marriage. Then I fled up the stairs and said, "If you don't like them, you may burn them."

STEVE: Oh, yes. Browning called them the finest sonnets since Shakespeare.

ELIZABETH: Too generously. Robert was a much finer poet than I. After much persuasion I allowed him to publish them under the title *Sonnets, from the Portuguese.* I did this on purpose, since I hoped the public would think them a translation and thus protect my privacy.

STEVE: Surely one of the most popular love poems ever written is in this collection. Let me see if I can remember it. *(Begins poem, halting a little)*

"How do I love thee,
Let me count the ways . . ."

ELIZABETH: *(She joins in and finishes alone.)*
I love thee to the depth and breadth and height
My soul can reach, when feeling out of sight
For the ends of Being and ideal Grace.
I love thee to the level of every day's
Most quiet need, by sun and candlelight.
I love thee freely, as men strive for Right;
I love thee purely, as they turn from Praise.
I love thee with the passion put to use
In my old griefs, and with my childhood's faith.
I love thee with a love I seemed to lose
With my lost saints—I love thee with the breath,
Smiles, tears, of all my life!—and, if God choose,
I shall but love thee better after death.

STEVE: "I shall but love thee better after death."

MACHIAVELLI: *Magnifico!!*

ARISTOTLE: Did you ever see your father again?

ELIZABETH: I wrote him regularly and in every letter begged his forgiveness. Robert and I made two trips to London, bringing Penini with us.

SUN: What did he think of his first grandson?

ELIZABETH: The servants were instructed to turn us away.

SUN: That's incredible.

ELIZABETH: My health began to fail again. We returned to Pisa.

STEVE: And you heard nothing from your father? At all?

ELIZABETH: Shortly after our return to the Continent Robert received a packet containing all the letters I had written Papa over the years, imploring his forgiveness. Not one of them had been opened. The seals were still intact.

Not long after that, my father died. When I heard the news, I collapsed. Gradually I stopped writing. My opium kept me asleep most of the time. I became weaker. Robert had to carry me everywhere.

In 1861—I was fifty-five—I died, in Robert's arms.

But oh, how I regret that my dearest Papa never got to know Robert, a son-in-law of whom he could have been so very proud! And that our darling son Penini also never knew his grandfather, who could have loved him so much.

STEVE: Well, thank you, Mrs. Browning, for sharing with us—*(Starts to turn to other guests)*

ELIZABETH: *(Sob.)* The letters! He never read my letters. He never forgave me. He never said good night. I loved him—Papa, I love you, dearest Papa. *(Crying, she exits up stairs, like a child.) (Aristotle rises and moves a step upstage, looking at Elizabeth's departing figure.)*

STEVE: Gentlemen, will you join us next time for a continuation of our discussion?

SUN: Certainly, Mr. Allen. *(All rise.)*

STEVE: Thank you. Good night.

SHOW # 16

Aristotle
(BERNARD BEHRENS)

Niccolo Machiavelli
(ALFRED RYDER)

Elizabeth Barrett Browning
(JAYNE MEADOWS)

Sun Yat-Sen
(KEYE LUKE)

Welcome again to Meeting of Minds.

Our guests—returning this evening for a continuation of their discussion are:

From Greece of the third century B.C. . . . the philosopher Aristotle.

From sixteenth-century Italy . . . Niccolo Machiavelli.

From nineteenth-century England . . . poet Elizabeth Barrett Browning.

And from twentieth-century China . . . Sun Yat-Sen.

And now—your host—Mr. Steve Allen.

STEVE: Thank you. Good evening. Well, our last program was particularly exciting, thanks to our four visitors from the past. Aristotle naturally told us something of Greek philosophy, and of his personal experience as tutor to Alexander the Great.

Niccolo Machiavelli, whose views horrify all political idealists, and whom Christians—among others—consider the philosopher of modern totalitarianism—nevertheless defended his opinions quite heatedly, as he seems to be doing at the moment.

Sun Yat-Sen, founder of the first Chinese Republic, told us something of the drama of twentieth-century China.

And Elizabeth Barrett Browning—in recalling the moving story of her long illness, irrational domination by her father, and her escape to the loving protection of poet Robert Browning, became— well, overwrought and left our discussion in tears.

ARISTOTLE: I do hope the dear lady will be joining us.

SUN: Yes, indeed.

STEVE: I honestly don't know if she will. I hope I don't sound like a male chauvinist, but women—at least of Mrs. Browning's sort— are so emotional that—well, now wait. Perhaps I'm making an unwarranted assumption here.

ARISTOTLE: Um hummm.

STEVE: Would you gentlemen agree that women are more emotional than men?

ARISTOTLE: Let us define the term *emotional,* if we can. The emotions are strong feelings that produce motion—that move us to behave in one way or another. We refer to fear, anger, love, sexual desire, jealousy.

STEVE: Do women feel these more than men?

ARISTOTLE: As for sexual appetite it is stronger in the male.

MACHIAVELLI: Not in my experience.

SUN: I would think that as regards the other emotions, however, men and women feel them in equal degree.

STEVE: But perhaps women reveal emotions more than men. A man may try to keep a stiff upper lip, as the British say.

MACHIAVELLI: A British man might do so. We Italian men certainly reveal our emotions freely.

ARISTOTLE: It is stimulating to see you gentlemen approach this question in so reasonable a way, for it is by such methods that we may discover the pure gold of truth. And after all, what distinguishes man from all other creatures is that he is the rational— or philosophical—animal. It is that ability of mind—and nothing else—that makes one a human being.

STEVE: Aristotle, since the subject of your philosophy has come up here, I'd like to—

MACHIAVELLI: May I risk seeming rude?

STEVE: (He smiles.) If you wish.

MACHIAVELLI: Thank you. You see, I want to suggest that, before you put more questions to Aristotle about his philosophy, you would be well-advised to sketch out something of the historical background from which Aristotle emerged. I mean this not only in the sense of the history of the politics of Greece before and during his time, but—even more importantly—in terms of the dimensions of philosophy itself before Aristotle.

STEVE: You're absolutely right.

MACHIAVELLI: Scholars, of course, are aware of the incredible contribution to modern-day civilization made by ancient Greece, but I wonder if the average man really has the remotest conception of the importance of what the Greeks achieved. There have been hundreds of city-states, tribes, peoples, nations, down through history, but a surprisingly small percentage of them have left any important imprint upon the ages that followed.

SUN: And just think: The achievements of Athens took place during a brief two-hundred-year period!

MACHIAVELLI: Si.

ARISTOTLE: Yes. Intellectually Greece achieved more in two-hundred years than the Egyptian empire did in five-thousand years!

STEVE: (To Machiavelli) It is, as you say, Machiavelli, an incredible achievement. Perhaps we should try to put it in historical perspective. What do we know of the origin of the Greeks?

ARISTOTLE: Well, I rather like the observation that I understand Attila the Hun made in one of your discussions when he suggested that nothing really is known about the origin of any people. The rea-

son, of course, is that such a long period of time has elapsed, for
all of us, that the tribal beginnings—if it is proper to use that word
at all—are hopelessly lost in the mists of antiquity.

SUN: Perhaps, when it was still possible to suppose that man had been
on this earth for just a few thousand years, it seemed sensible to
talk of the beginnings of peoples, but it is interesting to note that
the stories about such beginnings are always mythical in character.

MACHIAVELLI: That is certainly true of China.

ARISTOTLE: *(To Steve)* But let us go back—arbitrarily—to about two-
thousand years before Christ, to use your calendar, though naturally your Bible did not exist. The civilization of Crete was influential in the Mediterranean area at the time. Certain tribes were
migrating from northern and eastern areas down toward the warmer Mediterranean. There were local inhabitants of the area now
called Greece, of course, but again, nothing is known of their origin.

MACHIAVELLI: Even you Athenians knew nothing about them?

ARISTOTLE: Nothing at all. For several centuries there was a great
intermingling of peoples. There was an early stage when something
advanced enough to be called civilization began to appear in the
Greek areas, but it was wiped out by one of the massive Aryan
invasions that swept down the mountain passes. The invaders
fought with iron weapons, and the Greeks—badly defeated—were
set back to the early stages of ignorance and barbarism. *(Steve
shakes head.)*

By 1000 B.C. the first stage of European civilization in Greece—
which was largely Cretan in influence—had vanished. But now the
survivors of the Greek culture began to congregate gradually on
the islands, and on the coast of Asia Minor, and within a few
centuries they had given rise to a new and even more remarkable
civilization.

MACHIAVELLI: Yes. It is at about *this* time that many of the great names
of early Greek literature, science, and philosophy began to appear.

STEVE: For example?

MACHIAVELLI: Homer, Hesiod, Democritus, Thales, Sappho, Pytha-
goras.

STEVE: You know, Mrs. Browning had such an interest in Greek
philosophy and literature it's a shame she's not here.

ARISTOTLE: Where is she?

STEVE: I'll go look. I believe she was in the library just a few minutes
ago. *(He leaves.)*

ARISTOTLE: Perhaps Mrs. Browning became so upset by our questioning of her last time that she. . . .

STEVE: *(Entering, to Elizabeth)* Yes, I wish you would.

ELIZABETH: Very well.

STEVE: Gentlemen, it seems Mrs. Browning became so involved with our books that she didn't notice the time.

ELIZABETH: Forgive me, gentlemen. I found the most beautiful edition of Robert's poetry.

SUN: Mrs. Browning, we had just started to speak of the philosophers and poets of ancient Greece, and a question occurred to me. Since you and your husband were both poets, did you ever feel competitive?

ELIZABETH: Never! Robert's poems were far superior to mine.

STEVE: That is very generous of you.

ELIZABETH: I am not being generous, sir. I simply recognize the verdict of a later age. The public of my own time—and many critics as well—foolishly thought I was the better poet.

STEVE: Is that right?

ELIZABETH: Yes. This angered me greatly. It was so unjust to Robert. But he never complained.

I'm so glad to have the opportunity to speak of Robert's poetry. It was so beautiful.

SUN: You are a very dutiful wife, Mrs. Browning.

ELIZABETH: Oh, no, Dr. Sun. The whole world thrills to Robert's poems. I was just rereading *Pippa's Song*. How could anyone read it, or hear it, for that matter, without smiling? *(Reading from book.)*

The year's at the spring,
And day's at the morn;
Morning's at seven,
The hill-side's dew-pearl'd;
The lark's on the wing;
The snail's on the thorn;
God's in His Heaven—
All's right with the world!

STEVE: Speaking of critics, I understand that after your elopement William Wordsworth said, "So Robert Browning and Miss Barrett have gone off together! I hope they can understand each other. Nobody else can."

ELIZABETH: *(She laughs.)* Yes. Many people found Robert somewhat obscure. And in all honesty . . . once he was asked about the meaning of a particularly troublesome passage in his beautiful poem

Sordello. He said, "When I wrote that, only God and Robert Browning knew what it meant . . . Now . . . only God knows."

But much of Robert's work was not obscure at all. What could be more simple than *Home Thoughts from Abroad*—why, almost every schoolchild knows it by heart.

Oh, to be in England
Now that April's there,
And whoever wakes in England
Sees, some morning, unaware,
That the lowest boughs
  and the brush-wood sheaf
Round the elm-tree bole
  are in tiny leaf.
While the chaffinch sings
  on the orchard bough
In England—now!

And who can resist the clear simple beauty of. . . .
Grow old along with me!
The best is yet to be,
The last of life for which the
first was made:
Our times are in His hand
Who sayeth the whole I plan, youth
shows but half
(Trust God; see all nor be afraid.)

STEVE: Most people today don't realize what a productive period your age was for writers. We haven't time to name them all but consider. Among Mrs. Browning's contemporaries were: Edgar Allen Poe, Charles Dickens . . .

ELIZABETH: George Elliot, The Brontë Sisters . . .

STEVE: Harriet Beecher Stowe . . .

ARISTOTLE: Honore Balzac . . .

STEVE: Nathaniel Hawthorne . . .

ELIZABETH: Lord Alfred Tennyson, William Wordsworth . . .

SUN: Victor Hugo . . .

STEVE: William Makepeace Thackeray . . .

MACHIAVELLI: Dante Gabriel Rosseti, Thomas Carlyle. . . .

ELIZABETH: And George Sand!

SUN: Why is it, do you think, so many great writers emerged at that time?

ARISTOTLE: I've found writers—especially poets—to be unusually sensitive people: They feel the underlying currents, the tensions of the times more clearly than most of us do.

MACHIAVELLI: And the nineteenth century was a time of great social upheaval.

ARISTOTLE: So I understand, and since writers have the gift of creativity, they are able to express their reactions and insights. Poetry is a remarkable art. It may concentrate into a few words a wide spectrum of emotion.

STEVE: What issues of your day moved you to take pen in hand, Mrs. Browning?

ELIZABETH: One was the immoral treatment of children in England's factories. *(To Steve)* And in your own as well.

MACHIAVELLI: Immoral, how so?

ELIZABETH: You have no idea, *signore*, how disgraceful, how inhuman, were the conditions in which poor children had to work in the industrial society of the nineteenth century. Little boys and girls working at complicated, dangerous machines, their fingers in constant danger of being chopped off. "Oh, they seldom lose a whole hand," one of the overseers said, "and it's all due to the carelessness of the children." And children, you know, were put to work in coal mines in those days!

MACHIAVELLI: Really? At what ages?

ELIZABETH: Five or six.

ARISTOTLE: How could anyone force so young a child to work in a mine?

SUN: Greed is a powerful motive, my friend.

ELIZABETH: Where the passageways were too small for grown men, the children were forced to pull heavy carts of coal, crawling on their hands and knees, through pitch-dark, foul smelling passages.

SUN: How long did they work each day?

ELIZABETH: Sometimes as long as sixteen hours. On Sunday—their one day off—they were too tired to do anything but sleep. As if all that wasn't horrifying enough, the poor children were sometimes beaten by their overseers.

MACHIAVELLI: Did no one in your society try to protect them?

ELIZABETH: Oh, yes. But such "outside agitators," it was said, were interfering with the children's right to work.

SUN: Ah, it all sounds so familiar. The exploiters in China used the same heartless arguments.

ELIZABETH: The children were so stunted, so crippled, or diseased, that those who died young were considered fortunate. I was so angered by all of this that I wrote a poem, *The Cry of the Children.*

SUN: Would you please recite it for us?

ELIZABETH: I don't know if I can remember it.

STEVE: *(Opening book, flipping marked pages, shows it to her.)* I have it right here.

SUN: Would you read a passage for us?

ELIZABETH: *(Taking book.)* Very well.

Do ye hear the children weeping,
  O, my brothers,
Ere the sorrow come with years?
They are leaning their young heads
  against their mothers,
And that cannot stop their tears.
The young lambs are bleating in the meadows,
The young birds are chirping in the nest,
The young fawns are playing with the shadows,
The young flowers are blowing toward the west—
But the young, young children,
  O my brothers,
They are weeping bitterly!
They are weeping in the playtime of the others,
In the country of the free.
"True," say the children, "it may happen
That we die before our time:
Little Alice died last year, her grave is shapen
Like a snowball, in the rime.
We look into the pit prepared to take her:
Was no room for any work in the close clay!"
From the sleep wherein she lieth none will wake her,
Crying, "Get up, little Alice! It is day."
If you listen by that grave, in sun and shower,
With your ear down, little Alice never cries;
Could we see her face, be sure we should not know her,
For the smile has time for growing in her eyes:
And merry go her moments, lulled and stilled in
The shroud by the kirk-chime.
"It is good when it happens," say the children,
"That we die before our time."

MACHIAVELLI: Those are very moving sentiments, Mrs. Browning, but were you perhaps not indulging yourself? Would it not have been more productive to work for reform?

ELIZABETH: I do not want to appear boastful, *signore*, but this poem was responsible for arousing popular indignation, which in turn led to the passage of more humane child-labor laws.

MACHIAVELLI: I am glad to hear it.

SUN: Yes. The world now knows that the arts have great power to influence public opinion. Both Chiang Kai-Shek and Mao Tse-Tung were aware of this.

MACHIAVELLI: You know, Mrs. Browning, your poetry is beautiful, but, forgive me please, it's a pity that you devoted so much of your energy to the theme of romantic love and marriage.

SUN: Why would a European object to that, Machiavelli?

MACHIAVELLI: I am a product of the Italian Renaissance. We men of the Reniassance rarely thought of love and marriage as being necessarily combined.

STEVE: Really?

MACHIAVELLI: The story of Lorenzo de Medici makes the point. As a very young man he married Clarice Orsini, the daughter of an important family. He remained married to her; in fact she bore him several children. But at no time would it have occurred to him to love her.

STEVE: Incredible.

MACHIAVELLI: His first love was Lucrezia Danoti, a beautiful young Florentine girl whom Lorenzo loved so passionately that he wrote a number of sonnets for her. He subsequently had many other mistresses.

STEVE: With no sense of guilt?

MACHIAVELLI: Of course not. Most men of substance married for— er—social reasons, political, financial. . . . *(quietly)* Love . . . was . . . something else.

You remember, Aristotle, it was Demosthenes who said, "We have courtesans for the sake of pleasure, concubines for the daily health of our bodies, and wives to bear us lawful offspring."

SUN: And you consider all this compatible with Christianity?

MACHIAVELLI: *(An Italian* mezzo-mezzo *hand gesture)* Well. . . .

ELIZABETH: You have made your point, *Signore* Machiavelli, but I am comforted that the world much prefers my contention that love and marriage go together.

SUN: *(Gently)* Mrs. Browning, it might be a kinder world if your ideal were truly universally popular, but in China too—for many centuries—marriages were dictated by family or economic consiieration, and very rarely because of romantic love.

MACHIAVELLI: *Sì.*

STEVE: Yes, and today political factors are taken into account when a Chinese couple considers marriage.

But, speaking of romantic love, one of my favorite poems of yours, Mrs. Browning, is one of the sonnets, *If Thou Must Love Me.*

ELIZABETH: Now, that's one I don't recall word for word. Would you care to read it?

STEVE: Well, no, I—*Signore* Machiavelli, like men of the Renaissance generally, you were a lover of poetry.

MACHIAVELLI: I was more than that, sir. I wrote a certain number of poems.

STEVE: Marvelous. Then would you do us the honor of reading this one?

MACHIAVELLI: With pleasure. *(He reads.)*

If thou must love me, let it be for naught
Except for love's sake only. Do not say,
"I love her for her smile—her look—her way
Of speaking gently—for a trick of thought
That falls in well with mine, and certes brought
A sense of pleasant ease on such a day"—
For these things in themselves, Beloved, may
Be changed, or change for thee—and love, so wrought,
May be unwrought so. Neither love me for
Thine own dear pity's wiping my cheeks dry—
A creature might forget to weep, who bore
Thy comfort long, and lose thy love thereby!
But love me for love's sake, that evermore
Thou mayest love on, through love's eternity.
*(repeats in Italian) In rece Pero amami per l'amore d'amore
Se que sempre potri amar per centre
Per l'etermita d'amore. (He moves to Elizabeth and kisses her hand) Bellissimo!*

STEVE: Indeed, Dr. Sun, it's a pity we don't have time to discuss Chinese poetry.

SUN: Yes, *Li t'ai P'o.*

STEVE: Yes, which—like almost everything in China—has a long and honorable tradition. But I wonder if you could tell us about the famous—or infamous—kidnapping incident which occurred in London in 1896?

SUN: Very well. I was traveling at the time, as they say, for my health. You see, I had become sufficiently—er—visible to the Manchu government that my head was valued at $50,000. The price ultimately went to half a million dollars—a high compliment, but hardly a bargain.

Anyway, I was in London, on my way to church one Sunday, when I was overtaken by a fellow Chinese. He engaged me in conversation. A moment later, another man appeared. Before I knew it, the two of them had pushed and dragged me up some stairs and through the door of a palatial home overlooking a square. I felt like a character in *Alice in Wonderland:* I did not know where I was nor why I was there. I was locked in an upper room and left utterly alone. Several hours later, I was finally informed that I was a guest of the Imperial Chinese Legation.

ELIZABETH: Good Lord, you might have been killed.

SUN: Precisely. Suddenly, an Englishman appeared, a Sir Haliday Macartney.

STEVE: Ah, good. He had come to rescue you.

SUN: Quite the reverse; he was an attorney in the pay of my captors.

STEVE: Did you make any effort to escape?

SUN: None was possible. I attempted to write notes on scraps of paper and throw them into Weymouth Street below, but I could not. I begged the English servant boys who brought me food each morning to help.

MACHIAVELLI: The Chinese officials had English boys working for them?

SUN: Yes. Without them I might well have been tortured or executed and nobody would have known. At first, however, instead of helping me, the boys told the Legation officials of my efforts to escape or get messages out. Under threat of torture I was forced to sign a confession that I had entered the Legation of my own free will. Faced with torture and death, I believe I would have gone mad, had it not been for my abiding faith in Almighty God.

STEVE: How long were you kept there?

SUN: Twelve days.

MACHIAVELLI: How did you finally escape?

SUN: I appealed again to one of the serving boys. I told him that the Emperor of China wished to kill me because I was a Christian, and because I was striving to secure good government in China. I told him—every word true—what would happen to me if I did not escape.

STEVE: What would have happened?

SUN: I would have been shipped back to China, my ankles crushed, my eyelids cut off, and finally I would be hacked into small fragments so that no one could claim my mortal remains. I literally placed my life in that boy's hands! I begged him to help, in the name of God and in the name of the fair and just government of Great Britain.

STEVE: And he agreed?

SUN: He was afraid to do more than carry notes outside the Legation to my friends. Upon receipt of the messages, my friends immediately revealed my story to the newspapers. On the evening of my eleventh day of captivity the London *Globe* published a story about me under the headline: CHINESE REVOLUTIONARY KIDNAPPED IN LONDON. Within two hours, the square below my window was thronged by Londoners who were incensed that such a thing could happen in their city. The very next day, I was released. I was immediately surrounded by reporters and well-wishers who coveted details about my experience more anxiously than the Manchu government coveted my head.

STEVE: Well, I suppose one such experience was enough to—

SUN: Oh, that was only one of several times I narrowly escaped torture and death, Mr. Allen.

STEVE: Is that right?

MACHIAVELLI: Dr. Sun, I believe that you were not successful in your first attempt to overturn the government.

SUN: That is correct. Nor on our second or third . . . or eighth or ninth, for that matter. In fact, in the period between 1906 and 1911, we young revolutionaries tried no fewer than ten times. Each campaign failed.

ELIZABETH: Why?

MACHIAVELLI: Yes, why?

SUN: For several reasons. We lacked a sustained military effort against a better-trained and better-supplied Imperial army. We lacked adequate lines of communication. And—most importantly—we lacked funds.

MACHIAVELLI: *I capisco.*

SUN: But each time we suffered defeat, our determination increased! And, like a rock crumbling under drops of water, the Manchu government finally lost its ability to resist. It capitulated on our eleventh try.

STEVE: That was in 1911, and you were named the first provisional president of the Republic of China.

SUN: Yes. But from a great distance.

STEVE: Oh? What do you mean?

SUN: Well, you see, I was traveling through your country raising funds at the time. In fact, I was in—I believe it was St. Louis when I heard that simultaneous insurrections in a dozen districts had been successful and that I had been appointed president!

STEVE: Where had the first outbreak occurred?

SUN: In Wuchang.

STEVE: Ah, just across the Yangtze river from Hangkow.

SUN: *(Surprised)* Oh, you know the city?

STEVE: I've visited it.

SUN: Well, at the time of the uprising a young officer whose name you will recognize was our chief of staff, Mr. Allen.

STEVE: That would be Chiang Kai-Shek?

SUN: That is correct.

STEVE: But let's now move to the year 1912, when you arrived in China to accept your role as provisional president.

MACHIAVELLI: You were president for how many days, Dr. Sun?

SUN: Forty-three.

STEVE: Why so short a term?

MACHIAVELLI: Because he had no experience at running a government!

SUN: More importantly, sir, I had no army.

MACHIAVELLI: *(Laughs)* Ah, good! So you agree with Mao Tse-Tung that political power grows out of the barrel of a gun!

SUN: *(Ignoring Machiavelli)* In any event, Mr. Allen, I willingly resigned the presidency.

STEVE: Resigned?! Why?

SUN: To accept appointment in the provisional government as Director General of Transportation and Trade. You see, if China was to survive in the modern world it desperately needed transportation and communication systems.

MACHIAVELLI: *(In a supercilious manner)* But surely there was more to it than that, Dr. Sun. Are we to be treated to a display of Oriental inscrutability?

SUN: Perhaps, my friend, when—in some cases—the Oriental appears inscrutable—it is actually the case that the Occidental is insensitive.

China also needed to develop its industry to free itself from domination by foreign powers. I felt I could make a more significant contribution in the role of Director General of Transportation and Trade than I could as provisional president. China needed a leader who could command the widest possible support of the people.

It seemed at the time that such leadership could best be provided by General Yuan Shih-Kai.

STEVE: Who was Yuan Shih-Kai?

SUN: A military leader who had been highly influential in the Imperial government, but who had recently been removed from power because of the threat he represented to it. He was sympathetic to many of the aims of us revolutionaries, you see. I mistakenly believed that General Yuan could carry China through a provisional stage as we moved to full status as a constitutional republic!

MACHIAVELLI: But that did not happen, did it?!

SUN: No. The revolution had scarcely been completed when members of our own party differed on how reconstruction should proceed. My own plan—fashioned after thirty years of study and research—was deemed impractical, utopian.

ARISTOTLE: What was your plan, Dr. Sun?

SUN: I began with the premise that we must act or perish. And I believed that we could act to unite 450 million Chinese who were then like a loose, scattering, sheet of sand.

STEVE: A task easier defined than accomplished.

SUN: No, quite the reverse. But, in fact, my whole plan for reconstruction of China was paralyzed by the very belief you express.

MACHIAVELLI: But what were the details of your plan for China?

SUN: There were three principles to it. They were nationalism, *Min-Tsu Chu I*; people's rights, *Min-Chuan Chu I;* and people's livelihood, *Min-Cheng Chu I.* We meant to unite a whole nation, to achieve not only self-respect but also the respect of other countries.

STEVE: And China at that time was not respected by the major powers?

SUN: Not at all, Mr. Allen. Think of it! We were a great people, with a five-thousand-year history, a tradition of art, of philosophy, of scholarship and administration. Your own country then had a history of only some one-hundred-fifty years, but you Westerners treated us as if we were ignorant savages! Well, we revolutionaries meant to actualize Napoleon's prediction that when China finally awakened it would astound the world! By nationalism, we meant to free China from economic exploitation by outside forces, and to depend on our own resources.

STEVE: How?

SUN: By industrializing and developing communication and transportation systems.

MACHIAVELLI: And the second principle, Dr. Sun. What specifically did you mean by people's rights?

SUN: Very simple. We meant to have China ruled not by a powerful few, but by the people themselves! Consequently I wished all adult citizens to vote.

ELIZABETH: Including women?

SUN: Er—women in China in 1912, Mrs. Browning, were not considered citizens.

ELIZABETH: I see. Just as in your Athens, Aristotle.

STEVE: Women are permitted to vote in modern China.

SUN: Yes. And we meant to provide the people with the right of recall, the right of initiative, and the right of referendum—exactly as you had done in America.

STEVE: And as they do not do in the China of today.

SUN: Unfortunately, no.

ELIZABETH: An ambitious program, Dr. Sun, especially for a people so long kept in darkness and illiteracy by their former rulers.

SUN: When one believes in the practicability of a plan, Mrs. Browning, be it to move mountains—it can be accomplished! But when we permit ourselves to be convinced of impracticability—even in the case of such simple acts as moving one's hand—it cannot be carried out. So great is the power of the mind over behavior. You see, the men who thought my plan was utopian lacked conviction! China needed a republic, just as a child needs school. Because he does not know his letters—his words—must the child be deprived of school? Of course not. If he doesn't know the characters, he should set about learning them. Carrying out the unknown is the stimulus to development and progress!

ARISTOTLE: How true.

STEVE: And what did you mean by the third principle—people's livelihood?

SUN: You may prefer to call it socialism, sir. First of all, you must understand that nonsocialistic methods had had free reign in China for many centuries. As a result of free-economy methods hundreds of millions in China lived in abject poverty, ignorance, disease, and squalor. Now—we proposed to take great concentrations of economic power away from the rich and the selfish and the foreigners and to nationalize China's industries. We also planned to redistribute the land so that each poor peasant could own the soil on which he worked.

MACHIAVELLI: You planned to take their holdings away from the landlords?

SUN: Yes.

MACHIAVELLI: A grave mistake. A prince can commit any atrocity, carry out any reform, but at all costs, he must abstain from taking the property of his citizens.

STEVE: Why do you say that?

MACHIAVELLI: Because men are so greedy for material possessions that they forget more easily the death of their fathers than the loss of their inheritance.

ARISTOTLE: I find very little in what you have said so far, Machiavelli, that would suggest that you have a generous spirit. Is there no room for generosity in your prince?

MACHIAVELLI: (He smiles.) Oh, it would be well for the prince to be considered generous. But true generosity, as the world understands it, will injure him. If it is used virtuously and in the proper way, it will not be known. Better that the prince be thought miserly.

ARISTOTLE: Miserly?

MACHIAVELLI: Yes! If the prince wants to be known for generosity, he will consume all his resources and be forced to impose heavy taxes on his people if he wishes to maintain his reputation. But this taxation will make his subjects begin to hate him, and thus his reputation for generosity will be injured. If he is prudent, however, he will be thought miserly—and not be concerned about it. Because when he has sufficient revenue to defend himself against those who make war on him, and when he can undertake enterprises without burdening his people, he will be thought generous.

ARISTOTLE: Now let me sum up the particulars here. You have made an argument for the appearance rather than the reality of virtue.

MACHIAVELLI: But not without your instruction, amico.

ARISTOTLE: Oh? How is that?

MACHIAVELLI: Do you not recall writing that the king should collect taxes so that it appears they are used for state purposes . . . that he should not parade his vices but produce the impression that he is a statesman, even if he neglects certain virtues?

ARISTOTLE: Ah, but I said these were the ways of tyrants, Machiavelli. In the best political organization one cannot be a good king— or even a citizen—without being a good man.

MACHIAVELLI: But Aristotle, I say again—there never has been such a kingdom or republic. It has been created only in writing! In the gifted imaginations of such decent men as yourself!

ARISTOTLE: And in your imagination, you have created a monster of unrelenting pessimism . . . in the name of reality. And another thing: As Dr. Sun has already pointed out, the sexual behavior of the men of your day was hardly consistent with the Christianity you professed. And we have seen that your political views cannot possibly be justified within the context of Christian moral philosophy.

MACHIAVELLI: I did not invent fraud, treachery, or deceit, Aristotle. All of it was in the world long before either of us. The task of the prince is to learn to deal with it, not to philosophize it away.

SUN: Machiavelli, there will always come a time—if not simply the temptation—when the prince chooses to be cruel. If he is inconstant in his word, if he courts fear among his citizens to the point of hate, forgoing love—doesn't such conduct inevitably lead to the exercise of cruelty?

MACHIAVELLI: The prince must appear to be merciful, not cruel, Dr. Sun. But he must be careful not to misuse mercy.

ELIZABETH: Misuse it? How can one possibly misuse mercy?

MACHIAVELLI: By squandering it, my dear lady. But when cruelties are deemed necessary by the prince, they should be committed, all at once! And quickly.

STEVE: Quickly? Why?

MACHIAVELLI: There being less time to feel and worry about them, they therefore give less offense. On the other hand, favors should be dealt out a few at a time so that their effect may be more enduring. But treatment—cruel or kindly—should not vary with passing circumstance.

In times of adversity, when they seem most appropriate, cruelties often come too late, and whatever mercies the prince shows are of no use, since they will be thought of as being forced by the circumstance and he will receive no credit for them.

Hannibal, famous for bringing elephants through the snows of Europe, led an enormous army, composed of many races, that fought in foreign lands. No dissensions rose among them or against their prince, whether in good fortune or bad.

And do you know why things went so smoothly!? I shall tell you. Because of nothing else but Hannibal's inhuman cruelty! Without that cruelty, his other virtues would have been insufficient to his purpose!

The very safety of a country depends on such firmness! No consideration of justice or injustice, no consideration of glory or shame should be allowed to prevail! The only important question is what course will save the life and liberty of the country!

You, Dr. Sun, though you were an effective revolutionary, you—like Kerensky in Russia—were shortly swept aside by men who had a better grasp of the realities of political leadership!

ARISTOTLE: The ends, Machiavelli, do not justify the means.

MACHIAVELLI: Oh, of course they do! Why do all you pious moralists *lie* about this?!

SUN: You agree with Lenin on this point, Machiavelli.

MACHIAVELLI: Certainly, I grant that it would be most praiseworthy if all qualities accounted as good were found in the prince. But since they cannot be, the prince must be prudent enough to escape those vices which would result in the loss of his state, as you lost yours, my friend.

ARISTOTLE: It must amuse you, Dr. Sun, that the fierce and scarcely moral Europeans who began to force their way into China not long after Machiavelli's time considered the Chinese to be barbarians.

SUN: *(He laughs heartily.)* Yes. China did perceive the irony of this. But at the time of my troubles I was saddened that thirty years of faithfulness to the principles of nationalism, people's rights, and people's livelihood had been crushed.

STEVE: How?

SUN: General Yuan Shih-Kai betrayed our revolution and actually declared himself Emperor! More crises followed. Rioting and fighting continued long after I left the scene. But it was the reconstruction that failed, not the revolution.

ELIZABETH: *(Quietly)* Perhaps it happened because you loved the future more than the present, Dr. Sun.

STEVE: In reviewing your career, Dr. Sun, one historian wrote that you were a revolutionary leader whose success lay in continued defeat. Almost single-handedly you destroyed a corrupt monarchy and created a modern republic, with little more than a handful of students and a passionate belief in the divine right of men to govern themselves. With three words, you overturned a vast kingdom. An incredible accomplishment!

MACHIAVELLI: But in the end a failure. Despite its name China today is hardly a "modern republic" in the Western sense.

STEVE: But perhaps it is in your sense, Machiavelli.

MACHIAVELLI: What do you mean?

STEVE: Karl Marx called your *Florentine History* "a masterpiece." And the official *Encyclopedia of the Soviet Union* has therefore referred to you in complimentary terms. The Russian scholar Maximovich states that your concept of harsh, audacious dictatorship was in agreement with that of Lenin.

MACHIAVELLI: I am very honored.

ARISTOTLE: You have already told us enough, Machiavelli, for us to know that your so-called model prince can neither trust nor be trusted. Does it follow that the prince should not be loved and respected by his citizens, as Dr. Sun still is?

MACHIAVELLI: Where possible, he should be both, Aristotle. But it is much safer for the prince to be feared.

ARISTOTLE: A dismal prospect.

MACHIAVELLI: *(Ignoring him)* Men in general are dissemblers, ungrateful, anxious to avoid danger, eager for selfish gain. As long as you benefit them, they "bravely" promise to offer their blood, their goods, their children—when the need for them is remote.

SUN: And when it is not remote?

MACHIAVELLI: They will abandon you or revolt. The prince who relies solely on their words, without making other preparations, is ruined.

SUN: *Signore* Machiavelli, I understand that when Voltaire visited this table he observed that nice, loving people tend to believe in a nice, warm, loving God—whereas angry vindictive people tend to believe in an angry, vindictive God. It seems to me that the same is true concerning the two chief views of mankind.

STEVE: How do you mean?

SUN: Compassionate, friendly people tend to see humanity as basically good. Bitter, selfish people tend to see all humanity as bitter and selfish.

ELIZABETH: Quite so, Dr. Sun. But *Signore* Machiavelli, do you think there is no value to the love people may feel for a leader?

MACHIAVELLI: Such love, Mrs. Browning, is held by a chain of obligation which is broken whenever it serves the purpose of the lovers! Fear is maintained by the dread of inevitable punishment! A wise prince relies on what is in his power and not on what is in the power of others.

ARISTOTLE: No! Such a concept can never truly serve either the prince or the state.

MACHIAVELLI: Why not?

ARISTOTLE: Because it is based on vile views of human nature. The ideal situation is that in which a ruler possesses both the appearance and the reality of virtue. Even when men strive for perfection, they often fall short. But to set our sights as low as you recommend, my friend, is to make evil all the more certain!

SUN: Your cynicism, *Signore* Machiavelli, is depressing. Thank God most men consider your views immoral and destructive! Our friend Aristotle made a far more important contribution to philosophy and morality! And we are indebted to Aristotle, also, for his encouragement of reason.

ELIZABETH: Yes, Machiavelli! Once political practice is totally cut off from God's law, then the people have nothing whatever to protect them from brutality and despotism! One cannot possibly believe in human rights and at the same time accept your heartless philosophy.

STEVE: To put it in the language of the street, Machiavelli, you would agree with the American baseball manager who said, "Nice guys finish last."

MACHIAVELLI: They do in politics!

ARISTOTLE: A foolish generalization. If virtue is of so little value, my friend, then why is Dr. Sun Yat-Sen a hero to almost a billion people?!

MACHIAVELLI: Because he became a symbol! He helped free China from foreign domination. That made him a hero to the Chinese people—quite properly. But since his day his popularity, it seems to me, has been cynically exploited by both the Chinese Nationalists and their enemies, the Communists.

STEVE: Speaking of the high regard in which you are held, Dr. Sun, when I visited Nanking my son and I took photographs of the enormous memorial erected in your honor by the Nationalist government, now kept in good repair by the Communists.

SUN: Ah, yes. Thank you. I am deeply touched.

STEVE: The memorial is built along the side of a mountain and people come from all over the world to visit your tomb.

SUN: Thank you. But let us change the subject.

You know, it is easy to overlook the great importance of what Aristotle did in inventing the syllogism.

STEVE: Since we've been instructed about the importance of defining terms—Aristotle, what is a syllogism?

ARISTOTLE: It is, among other things, a formulation of words. These are words which express certain assumptions which, in turn—if accepted—inescapably lead to certain conclusions. The simplest possible sort of syllogism would be this: When A equals B, and B equals C, then it is absolutely, inescapably the case that A equals C.

STEVE: But isn't it simpler—and clearer—to talk about physical realities such as tables, apples, or whatever than to work problems out by manipulating abstract symbols such as A, B, X, or Y?

ARISTOTLE: There is no need, sir, to make an either/or choice here.

The advantage of the syllogism is that it expresses the relation of the terms to one another, without referring to any specific subject matter. A, B, C, or the other letters can represent anything you want them to. And no matter what you decide they represent, the thought sequence—the reasoning process—will be a good one so long as you keep A, B, and C in their proper relative places.

SUN: Yes. You see, the reason this seemingly simple concept of Aristotle's has been so vitally important down through the centuries is that he was the first person to have the idea of breaking up the process of thought itself into its separate parts.

ARISTOTLE: Thank you.

ELIZABETH: *(Partly putting them on)* But then, gentlemen, why do any of us think poorly at all anymore, if we've been taught to employ Aristotle's syllogism?

MACHIAVELLI: *(He chuckles.)* The danger, my dear, grows out of the fact that the initial premise—which, let us say, would be represented by the letter A, may itself be totally false. Therefore, you can end up with a conclusion which, though it is absolutely valid logically, is nevertheless nonsense.

SUN: I tend to agree with you, *signore.* Let us consider, for example, Mrs. Browning, the premise statement, "All Europeans are barbarians," which we will represent by the letter A. We know, of course, this is not so, but let us put it to use nevertheless. It was, in fact, fervently believed by the Chinese for centuries. Let us then arbitrarily make the second statement, or premise, "Barbarians are bad people." This leads—inescapably—to the conclusion—C—"All Europeans are bad people."

ELIZABETH: Yes, quite. As Machiavelli pointed out, the reasoning itself is perfectly sound but since the premises were false they led to a nonsensical conclusion.

SUN: Precisely.

ARISTOTLE: You may, in fact, have either one false premise or two false premises in a syllogism. We must be very careful indeed about the correctness of our premises. We must, in other words, *not* take these basic statements for granted but must examine them to see if they are, in fact, true.

MACHIAVELLI: This is particularly so in the areas of ethics, morals. Yet ethical and moral questions do not necessarily deal with fact. In other words, the question is not, Is there an apple on the table? but, Should there be an apple on the table?

ARISTOTLE: Yes. We refer here to opinion, what people think is the case as regards behavior.

ELIZABETH: You gentlemen seem to be pointing to a rather hopeless situation. Since matters of opinion cannot possibly have the certainty that matters of fact can, then is there any hope at all for thinking reasonably and logically about ethical questions?

ARISTOTLE: Yes, there is hope. You are quite right in assuming that we cannot be as certain about such things as we can about scientific questions. Therefore we turn for help to tradition.

STEVE: Tradition?

ARISTOTLE: Yes. You see Mr. Allen, what most people have thought about something over a very long period of time, while it is not necessarily true and wise, is nevertheless much more likely to be so than what some individual thinks up after just a moment's reflection.

SUN: But certainly you would not suggest, Aristotle, that an idea is valid simply because it is old. If I believed any such thing I would have never been able to found a republic in China. For in doing so, I had to go counter to much that was traditionally believed in my society.

ARISTOTLE: But even you—even Mao Tse-Tung—did not discard *all* of China's traditions.

SUN: Oh, no.

ARISTOTLE: But let us return to a point we discussed before, the danger of making careless generalizations that are simply accepted, rather than examined to see if they are—in fact—true. In doing so we must examine many cases—many instances—for if we find even one negative instance this means that our generalization does not hold water.

MACHIAVELLI: Yes. Science is one field, at least, in which there is an ongoing search for negative instances.

ARISTOTLE: Quite. But I doubt if the average person grasps one implication of this.

STEVE: And what is that, sir?

ARISTOTLE: That what we casually consider scientific truths—are, if we want to be strict about it, actually scientific generalizations concerning which no negative instances have as yet been encountered.

ELIZABETH: You know, gentlemen, something's just occurred to me. It's fascinating that in the world of science—where things can be measured and weighed and experimented with, and where the scientific generalizations you've mentioned, Aristotle, are almost certainly true—scientists, such as yourself, are nevertheless careful to qualify their assertions.

But in the field of religion—where it is very difficult indeed to determine anything at *all* in the factual sense—we find a great deal of firm conviction, a great many beliefs about which people feel absolutely certain.

ARISTOTLE: *(He laughs heartily.)* That is a very wise observation indeed, my dear. One thing it shows, of course, is the basic reason why there will always be some degree of conflict between the domain of science and that of religion.

MACHIAVELLI: Hmph, some degree of conflict indeed! It's frequently been actual warfare. For centuries the churches have used poison, the sword, the prison dungeon, the axe, and the fires of the stake as their weapons against scientists and others who advanced theories churchmen did not like.

ARISTOTLE: The crimes committed by the churches down through the ages, my friend, are horrible enough. But you Christians had no monopoly on them. Almost all religious groups have resorted to the most uncivilized methods in the heat of controversy.

SUN: Yes. As a Christian myself, I was always profoundly saddened by this tragic aspect of religious history.

ELIZABETH: And not only religions but governments as well.

ARISTOTLE: Of course!

STEVE: Doesn't that suggest, sir, the wisdom of teaching us how to think as early as we are taught how to read and write?

ARISTOTLE: You mean at a very early age?

STEVE: Yes. If you can teach a five-year-old child how to add, how to spell, how to draw, why can't you begin teaching him how to think at that age? I've been recommending this for twenty years. So far without much effect, I admit. Most adults don't reason very well, but I have the idea that if we were taught to reason in our childhood, we would be considerably less likely to become either religious or political fanatics in later life. And our religious or political views would be wiser.

ARISTOTLE: I am glad that you said "less likely," rather than suggesting that such evils could be totally done away with if all men knew how to reason.

ELIZABETH: You know, it is literally thrilling, Aristotle, to sit here and have you clarify for us some of the rudiments of thought. But can such lessons be applied to everyday life?

ARISTOTLE: Oh, absolutely, Mrs. Browning! Again, all of us are in the habit of making generalizations. Now, we cannot possibly stop,

sit down, and respond to each and every object that comes to our
attention. If we could freeze this moment of time *(He snaps his
fingers.)* and then go back and look into it we would see that there
are literally thousands of things to which we might have given
attention in that moment. Thousands of objects about us, people,
sights, colors, sounds. We hurry through life at such a speed that
we cannot constantly be responding to all the things about us. So
the human brain—or mind—has developed this capacity to
generalize, to make quick general judgments about things, about
conditions, that enables us to get a great deal done, so to speak.
But this has its unfortunate side in that it leads us to make rough
generalizations about—let us say—other human beings.

Men, for example, might make the generalization we mentioned
earlier, "All women are overly emotional." Now as long as we can
point to certain individual women who are not overly emotional
then the generalization has no value. Nevertheless, many people
who make such generalizations—and who never hear them
contradicted—gradually come to believe that they are speaking the
truth.

MACHIAVELLI: Oh, yes. And whoever tells them they are speaking
nonsense may pay dearly for his freedom of speech.

SUN: I would say—as a general rule—that we ought to be on guard
whenever we hear that word *all.*

ARISTOTLE: A very good idea, Dr. Sun. It is perfectly possible, of course,
to make true statements beginning with the word *all.* We can say,
for example, that all human beings are mammals. But that is a
simple scientific statement. As a general rule statements that began
with the word *all*—in everyday human discourse—ought to be
examined very carefully to see if they are reasonable or not.

ELIZABETH: Fascinating! I could listen to you clarify the process of
thought for hours, sir.

ARISTOTLE: Thank you, my dear, but it is quite frustrating to have
so little time to discuss a field of study that is so extended and
complex. Shall I continue?

STEVE and ELIZABETH: Oh, please.

ARISTOTLE: Very well. Consider next the important terms, *either/or*
and *not both.* If you are tossing a coin, for example, we know
that it must land either heads or tails. There are cases in which
something may be either this or that. But it may perhaps be both,
although not in precisely the same way or at the same time.

We might for example, say of this apple that it is either red or green. It obviously cannot be both at the same time. But it can be—and in fact has been—both red and green at different times.

But we are entitled to make what are called inferences. Simple, direct inferences.

STEVE: Could you comment on the word *inference*?

ARISTOTLE: Yes. This means that we infer something. To give a simple instance: When we toss the coin and see that it has landed heads up we are obviously permitted to make the simple, direct inference that the other side is still tails and that if, in fact, we have made a bet on the matter, and bet that it would land tails up, then we have lost that bet.

Let's us take the simple statement, "All grass is green." If we take that to be the case, then we also know immediately that some grass is green. We are also entitled to assume—to make the inference—that of all the green objects in the world, at least some of them are blades of grass. This—again—is what we call making inferences.

STEVE: But don't many of us make frequent mistakes with this seemingly simple process of inference?

ARISTOTLE: Indeed, we do make mistakes. For example, from the statement that "All grass is green," while it is perfectly correct to infer that some green objects are grass, it is not at all correct to infer that all green objects are grass. *(To Steve.)* Now you give me an example.

STEVE: All humans are mammals but we cannot say that all mammals are human.

ARISTOTLE: Correct. Another!

ELIZABETH: All Chinese are Orientals, but it would be a mistake to say all Orientals are Chinese.

ARISTOTLE: Good! Now I described that particular sort of mistake in thinking as an illicit conversion. The class of green objects, to return to my earlier example, is obviously much larger than the class of blades of grass. Grass is only one of the thousands of things in the world that are green. Cucumbers are green. Emeralds are green.

STEVE: Well, Aristotle, we're almost out of time. You had mentioned briefly earlier your relationship with the greatest military leader of your day. Could we ask for fuller details on that?

ARISTOTLE: Certainly. In the year 342 B.C. I was offered a very important post when King Philip II of Macedonia invited me to become the personal tutor to his son, Alexander.

STEVE: Was that considered a very unusual appointment in your day, for an important philosopher to serve as a tutor?

ARISTOTLE: No. It was the custom of the time to hire nothing less than philosophers to instruct the sons of kings.

STEVE: My goodness, how fortunate young Alexander was. *(To audience)* Can you imagine having Aristotle as your personal teacher?!

ARISTOTLE: I thank you for the implication of your question, but I do not regard my instruction of Alexander as a great success.

STEVE: Oh? Why?

ARISTOTLE: Well, the young fellow was—by nature—more interested in a life of action than in the world of thought. He cared—as became obvious—about military and political matters, and when his father, King Philip, died in 336 B.C., he began making his own plans to— well, to conquer the world.

STEVE: And you did not accompany him on his campaigns?

ARISTOTLE: No, I returned to Stagira, the town where I was born. About a year later I went back to Athens at which time I formed my own school, known as the Lyceum.

STEVE: Did you follow Plato's method of teaching there?

ARISTOTLE: Only to some extent. I was always inclined to organize, to try to make things orderly and systematic, so my school was somewhat less casual than Plato's had been. I usually lectured in the morning, when minds were fresh, and in the afternoon spoke on more popular matters, so as not to put the minds of my students under too much stress, and also to accommodate the many visitors from Athens who would come to hear me.

But, of course, open discussion was greatly encouraged. It is most unfortunate that many of your modern universities are so large that teachers simply have no time for discussion among students.

STEVE: Indeed. I understand you did not spend the rest of your life at your school. Why not?

ARISTOTLE: When Alexander the Great died—in 323 B.C.—this led to repercussions throughout the Greek world. One result was that I was no longer particularly welcome in Athens, because of my life-long ties to the Imperial court.

STEVE: That wasn't a crime, was it?

ARISTOTLE: No. The charge brought against me was the same that had been brought against Socrates, "impiety." Rather than have Athens sin twice against philosophy I turned my school over to my good friend Theophrastus and went to my mother's home in Chalcis. I died there, a year later, at the age of sixty-four.

STEVE: I imagine, sir, that in your last years thousands of people must have come to visit you—the greatest philosopher of your age.

ARISTOTLE: *(With wry humor)* There you go again, sir, with one of your damnable assumptions. But at least this time you did preface your observation with the phrase, "I imagine. . . ." I congratulate you on the vividness of your imagination, but the fact is that my last days were lonely. I was saddened to be separated from my school and I lived, for the most part, a very quiet life.

STEVE: Well, we in turn, sir, are saddened that so many of your writings have not survived the centuries. Fortunately Cicero and others who had the opportunity to read your early writings before they were lost have given us information about some of them, at least. Is it true in this connection, by the way, that you agreed with Plato's theory about the transmigration of souls? In other words, about reincarnation?

ARISTOTLE: Yes, I did.

STEVE: But isn't that a theory that—so far at least—it has not been possible to prove?

ARISTOTLE: Absolutely. That is why we call it only a theory. Perhaps the view came from my feeling that a soul is such an enormously important thing that God or the universe wouldn't waste it.

SUN: It is an ancient belief in the Orient.

ARISTOTLE: Yes, so I understand.

STEVE: When Plato was here, he discussed his theory of Ideas, that behind every actual object—every physical chair, or man, or table, or horse—there literally exists some perfect Idea of tables and chairs and men and horses, and so on.

ARISTOTLE: Yes, at one time I accepted that, but later the theory was not satisfactory to me. In my younger years I naturally tended to be more directly under the influence of Plato's powerful thought, but then with the passage of time I developed my own philosophical views. In the early period I was concerned with the unseen world of Platonic Ideas, but in time I became more passionately concerned about the physical realities, the things, the facts, of this world we live in.

I was, in that sense, a scientist. I collected examples of plants and animal life and classified them, and tried to think reasonably about them. I am pleased—indeed astounded—by the scholarly progress in the sciences in the present age. Modern science seems able to do almost anything. Science cannot, however, always deal satisfactorily with religious or moral questions. Science can tell us

how life works, but precisely what life is—precisely how it began—
of that we know nothing.

SUN: Science can, however, tell us that some theories about the beginning of life are absurd.

STEVE: Science can also tell us that we're out of time, as it does at
the moment. Thank you, Mrs. Browning; thank you, gentlemen,
for joining us, and *(to audience)* thank you for doing the same.

SHOW # 17

William Shakespeare
(HARRIS YULIN)

Woman
(JAYNE MEADOWS)

Hamlet
(ANTHONY COSTELLO)

Othello
(WILLIAM MARSHALL)

Romeo
(CHARLES LANYER)

Iago, Ghost
(FRED SADOFF)

Welcome again to Meeting of Minds, in which various distinguished
figures from different periods of history come together to exchange
views on important questions. The special theme of our program
this evening entitles us to call it "Shakespeare on Love."

And now . . . here is your host, Mr. Steve Allen.

STEVE: Thank you and welcome again. This evening's Meeting of Minds
is going to be a bit unusual; I just have that feeling. You see, through
my regular contacts in the, well, Great Beyond, I had extended
an invitation to William Shakespeare, which he kindly accepted.

I had thought it might be interesting to have Tolstoy as another
guest, since he had been so critical of Shakespeare. And a few
other ideas along that line had occurred to us here. But then I
began to receive strange messages that certain other personages
wished to appear with Shakespeare. It's been a very odd situation,
and the upshot of it is that we are not quite certain—even now—
just who the other guests are going to be. Perhaps Shakespeare
himself will resolve the mystery for us. We'll see.

Or, inasmuch as Shakespeare is considered by many to be both
the world's greatest poet and also the greatest dramatist, it might
be worthwhile to simply interview him alone for our first hour,
and just hope for the best as regards part two of our discussion.

You will note that I did not make the flat statement that
Shakespeare was the greatest dramatist and the greatest poet. I
said he was considered so "by many." That raises an interesting
point that emerged from our recent conversation with Aristotle,
Sun Yat-Sen, Elizabeth Barrett Browning, and Machiavelli, that
in assessing any personage from past ages we generally take into
account the final verdict of history and consequently overlook the
fact that not only during their lifetimes, but even subsequently, the
world jury that voted that verdict was by no means unanimous.

If there were such a thing as a planet all inhabitants of which
were purely rational, this would very probably not be the case.
But, as we know to our sorrow, ours is a planet on which the
light of pure, sweet reason glows very feebly and fitfully. What
this means as regards critical judgments—of almost anything—
is that the judges bring to the moment of their criticism an enormous baggage of nonrational considerations, among which are
their own philosophical biases and social prejudices, not to mention personal idiosyncracies, neuroses, loves, hates, and fears.
Whatever.

As one consequence of this we find that even the great figures of history—whether they were artists, philosophers, saints, or seers—have been subjected to far more criticism than the average person would receive in a hundred lifetimes. Most of us have to be content with criticism from our loved ones, friends, and acquaintances, whereas the great of the world are honored by the slings and arrows of millions.

As for Shakespeare, he'll have no trouble with me. I share the dominant critical view that he was a genius with dazzling gifts as poet and dramatist. Considering the degree of his eminence, it's odd that very little is known about his personal life.

One of the reasons for this, I suppose, is that in his own time, he was not nearly as big a deal as we now understand him to have been. Consequently, the biographers of his age, though they scrupulously recorded the doings of other figures of Elizabethan England, didn't pay much attention to Shakespeare.

Well, hopefully this evening we'll learn more, right from the horse's mouth. Speaking personally, I can hardly wait. Ladies and gentlemen, it is an honor indeed to introduce . . . *(laughs)* William Shakespeare. *(Superimpose: William Shakespeare 1564–1616)* How do you do, Mr. Shakespeare?

SHAKESPEARE: How do I do? I do as well as I might be expected to do, given the circumstances of my strange estate.

STEVE: How do you perceive those circumstances?

SHAKESPEARE: Why, I've been summoned from the privacy we find when freed from bounds of time and space,
not knowing what I might expect
but tempted by the lure of fresh experience. Please.

STEVE: Incredible. You choose to address us in iambic pentameter?

SHAKESPEARE: As the spirit moves me.

STEVE: The spirit that moved you, sir, must have been one with remarkable powers. As the word *inspiration* itself shows, you know, the ancients believed that remarkable creativity—in the arts—was not something for which the individual himself was responsible but rather that spirits—in the literal sense—inspired—breathed into the artist the dazzling conceptions which he then gives to the world. How do you feel on this observation?

SHAKESPEARE: The first man who thought that must have been either a remarkably humble artist or an envious critic. But this flower of ancient Greek speculation has taken no lasting root in Christian soil. A genius does his own hard work.

Perhaps the theory of literal inspiration grew out of the artist's own inability to understand the source of his creativity. None of us has ever known where his special gifts come from.

STEVE: What can you tell us of your family?

SHAKESPEARE: My father, John Shakespeare, was a civic official of Stratford. He was by trade a glover and—

STEVE: A glover?

SHAKESPEARE: Yes, he made gloves.

STEVE: It never before occurred to me that the name Glover—Mr. Glover—was simply that of a tradesman.

SHAKESPEARE: Oh, yes. This is true of many common English names, Mr. Tailor, Mr. Cotter,

STEVE: Mr. Glazier,

SHAKESPEARE: Mr. Cooper,

STEVE: Mr. Farmer.

SHAKESPEARE: Yes. My father had some experience at farming, by the way.

STEVE: It would be interesting to know more about your father's family.

SHAKESPEARE: Why?

STEVE: Well, it might enable us to understand you better.

SHAKESPEARE: How?

STEVE: Well, I don't know, really.

SHAKESPEARE: Nor do I.

STEVE: Well, the heck with it then.

SHAKESPEARE: Perhaps you would pluck out the heart of my mystery, eh?

STEVE: If I could. . . .

SHAKESPEARE: Are you implying that my abilities were somehow inherited from a talented progenitor? People assume that such speculation "explains" genius. It does nothing of the kind. It simply passes the question along to an earlier point in time. I know of no evidence that genius is inherited, though intelligence may be.

STEVE: Perhaps a genius is some sort of fortunate freak.

SHAKESPEARE: I wouldn't be surprised.

STEVE: Where you your parents' only child, sir?

SHAKESPEARE: No, I had three brothers, four sisters. But enough of that. I remember in 1577—I believe I was thirteen years old at the time—my father suffered certain financial reverses. This led in turn to a curtailment of my education.

STEVE: Too bad. I understand, though, you were married while still quite a young fellow.

SHAKESPEARE: Oh, yes, at age eighteen to one Anne Hathaway.

STEVE: A girl of your own age?

SHAKESPEARE: No, she was some eight years my senior. Or should I say my seniora? A very bad joke, wasn't it?

STEVE: Yes. You used to do a number of those, if you don't mind my saying so.

SHAKESPEARE: No. It's quite all right. Everyone is his own critic.

STEVE: Well, now, history knows that you subsequently left the town of Stratford.

SHAKESPEARE: Yes, it was 1584, as I recall. I'd gotten into a bit of a scrape in town, you know, and decided to see something of the world. London seemed an obvious choice. That was—after all—where the theatrical companies were.

STEVE: Yes. There would, as you say, have been theater productions in London in your youth. But had any traveling companies reached the smaller market town of Stratford?

SHAKESPEARE: Oh yes, indeed, and from my first exposure I was—as *you* say—stage-struck. I didn't at first know whether I wanted to act, write, to carry messages, or what. I only knew that the theater was to be my rightful home. It was in my twenties that I began to try my hand as a playwright.

STEVE: With what results?

SHAKESPEARE: Nothing notable at first. Actually, I didn't quite know what it was I wanted to write. A lot of the original impetus, I suppose, came from the simple feeling—after I had seen a few plays—that I might do better.

STEVE: You know, sir, one problem with interviewing you is that one hardly knows which of you to address. You are, after all, not only poet and dramatist, as the world knows, but very much a philosopher, psychologist, prophet, language-maker, musician, actor.

SHAKESPEARE: Ah, actor. Yes I was.

STEVE: In fact, I understand that among your various roles was that of the father's ghost in *Hamlet*.

SHAKESPEARE: Yes. the company seemed determined to restrict me to smaller parts; I don't know why that actually was.

STEVE: They wanted to keep you writing, perhaps.

SHAKESPEARE: Yes, perhaps. Let's hope so. Which of me will you choose?

STEVE: Well, I'll tell you. Another self, the lover. Or at least the one that knows of love. That's the one subject we'd like, or love, to hear you discourse on this evening.

SHAKESPEARE: *(He chuckles.)* Quite an order, I must say.

Lovers you know and madmen have such seething brains,
such shaping fantasies, that apprehend
more than cool reason ever comprehends.
The lunatic, the lover, and the poet
are, of imagination, all compact:
One sees more devils than vast hell can hold.
That is the madman. The lover, all as frantic,
sees Helen's beauty in a brow of Egypt:
The poet's eye, in a fine frenzy rolling,
doth glance from heaven to earth, from earth to heaven;
and, as imagination bodies forth
the shapes of things unknown, the poet's pen
turns them to shapes, and gives an airy nothing
a local habitation and a name.

I find myself curious, my good fellow, to know just who it is I am to meet here this evening. Did I understand you, a moment ago, to mention Tolstoy?

STEVE: Yes, but I don't believe he'll be joining us.

SHAKESPEARE: Good. I'm very relieved. Yes, Tolstoy is supposedly quite an opinionated fellow, and I understand that his opinions of me were not the most flattering. But if not Tolstoy—then who?

STEVE: Well, that's just it. Ordinarily, I make decisions about our guest list myself, but in this instance the situation seems to have gotten rather out of hand.

SHAKESPEARE: I don't understand.

STEVE: I don't either. But you see— *(There is a knocking at the door to the right.)* I—Excuse me, for a moment. I'm not quite sure—

SHAKESPEARE: Well, this is very strange, I must say. Unless there is a market for suspense the situation does not seem promising.

STEVE: *(Offstage)* Yes!

WOMAN: Is he in there?

STEVE: Yes.

WOMAN: May I enter?

STEVE: Well, not just yet. Would you excuse me for just a moment? *(He enters, closing door, and returns quickly to table.)* Oh dear! Mr. Shakespeare, if you will excuse me, our next guest is—at least I think she is—the Dark Lady of the Sonnets.

SHAKESPEARE: Oh, my God!

STEVE: Is anything wrong?

SHAKESPEARE: I do not want to see that woman!

STEVE: But she seems determined to see *you,* sir.

SHAKESPEARE: She always was remarkable for her determination, if little else. Well, if she's coming, I am *going*.

STEVE: Oh no, please. First of all, I'm not sure that the lady *is* the one to whom you wrote your famous sonnets and—*(Woman bangs the doors open and hurries into the room.)*

WOMAN: Ah, there you are, sweet William.

SHAKESPEARE: Now, see here. I wasn't told you were going to be here!

WOMAN: And what if you had been told? Your vanity would still have brought you here! So you're going to talk about love, are you?

SHAKESPEARE: And why not? Our Lord himself tells us it's the greatest of the virtues.

WOMAN: It's certainly the only one we repent.

SHAKESPEARE: *(To Steve)* Sir, I did not agree to this, and I'm not going to submit to it! *(He exits.)*

STEVE: *(Following him off.)* Sir, there are millions watching at the moment. I'm sure they'd be terribly disappointed if you—excuse me, madame. *(He exits.)*

WOMAN: My name is Woman.

STEVE: *(Offstage)* Is anything wrong? *(Men's voices trail off.)*

WOMAN: Cowards! *(She acknowledges the audience.)* Love, hah!
Of love you'd learn what Will Shakespeare has said?
(Sarcastically.) He knew little more when alive than dead.
You think: How dare I show him disrespect?
Well, let me some disjointed thoughts connect.
This much I'll say for Will: He was a man.
And that's the worst that *anyone* can say.
He laughed and wept, went contrary to plan.
Was weak in virtue, prone to disarray.
He was a bit of all things to all men.
I'm not impressed because I knew him when.
I know; with words he had a wondrous power.
I do not criticize a line he wrote.
He dropped sweet verses from his ivory tower.
But his smooth words on love stick in my throat.
There's plenty I could tell you, if I would.
No doubt you'd do the self-same if you could.
But I'm onstage and you are in your seats.
And so I'll have to call the turn, my sweets.
But now to business. It's your business too
to learn what foolish things we are, and do.
To learn of love is so to learn of life.

Come lover, maid. Come husband, mistress, wife.
Attend to Will's poor creatures: princes, kings.
Adventurers who'll tell of many things.
But chiefly love in various disguise,
of love grown dull, or taken by surprise,
of lust, of passion, innocent and wild
wherefore Adonis dreamed or Venus smiled.
I am one Woman and I am them all;
Dear lords and ladies, I stand at your call.
To serve my Romeo, Hamlet, or my Moor,
to be considered virgin, yes, and whore.
And all for love, this wondrous something rare
that seems as insubstantial as thin air.
But call it nothing? Never. Say not so.
Are smiles nothing that love brings to glow?
Is whispering nothing?
Is leaning cheek to cheek? Is meeting noses?
Kissing with inside lip? Stopping the career
of laughter with a sigh? A note infallible
of breaking honesty, horsing foot on foot?
Skulking in corners? Wishing clocks more swift?
Hours, minutes? Noon, midnight? And all eyes
blind with the pin and web but theirs, theirs only,
that would unseen be wicked? Is this nothing?
Why, then the world and all that's in't is nothing,
The covering sky is nothing; our planet nothing;
my life is nothing; nor nothing have these nothings,
if this be nothing.

But let us see what wisdom on the theme of love
poor William put in his creatures' mouths.
Who would you? Hamlet? Romeo? Othello?
So't shall be.
But ah—here come our lovers now. Mark them well.
Hope they remember what they have to tell.
(She makes a sweeping gesture of conjuration accompanied by music.)
HAMLET: *(He enters, reading silently, then looks about.)*
                                Ay, there's the rub,
    for in that sleep of death what dreams may come,

when we have shuffled off this mortal coil,
must give us pause. *(He chuckles dryly.)*

So once I thought . . . But when at last I slipped
into the airy realm that men call death
my fate, I found, no heaven was, nor hell.
I was condemned, for having wasted life,
to endlessly relive it, till the day
the last man burns my record, and forgets.
And so I wander through this lonely world,
crawling beneath my heaven and my earth,
still, like the whore, unpack my heart with words,
in ev'ry language and in ev'ry clime,
punished, for my sins, with too much time.

WOMAN: Among those sins, sir, if I may remind,
was your harsh treatment of Ophelia.
She did not any wrong. Rather than wife,
you chose to make her waster of her life! *(She gestures again
to summon Romeo. He enters, as if waking from a dream. Woman
exits.)*

ROMEO: What do you read, good sir?

HAMLET: *(Still puzzled, he looks after the departed Woman.)* Words,
words, words.

ROMEO: *(Sarcastically)* Proving a factual answer's not always the best.
What do the words *convey?*

HAMLET: Ideas and actions.

ROMEO: Have you a preference 'twixt the two?

HAMLET: Why, like yourself I'd be a man of action, but—
My intellect inhibits what I do. *(Laugh)*
Thus conscience doth make cowards of us all;
and so I circle once again to words.

ROMEO: *(With a smile)* In truth 'twould be too quiet here without them.
Your name, sir?

HAMLET: Hamlet, prince of Denmark.

ROMEO: Your servant, sir. *(He makes a small bow.)*

HAMLET: I need none. May you serve as friend in time.

ROMEO: I well could use a friend in this strange spot.

HAMLET: What? Strange to you as well? Where are we then?

ROMEO: Why, out of time and out of place, I'd say.

HAMLET: The mood is odd and yet familiar. *(He looks about.)* One
thing is clear, all *this* world's a stage. Could we be ghosts?

ROMEO: *(He laughs.)* Speak for yourself. I know I'm not. I'm real as ever was.

HAMLET: And what's reality?

ROMEO: *(He playfully draws his weapon.)* I'm sure, my Lord, you'd testify 'twas real

If in between your ribs I slipped this steel.

HAMLET: *(He laughs.)* Thus driving home your point, my friend, too well.

You would indeed prove flesh and blood exist,

but what of spirits?

ROMEO: *(With a shrug)* Call an exorcist! *(He turns to Hamlet.)* Why are we here?

HAMLET: *(With a slight wry smile)* A question never rightly answered through all time.

Your name, sir?

ROMEO: Romeo Montague, of Verona.

HAMLET: Why, what have we in common?

ROMEO: Everything, my Lord. Except for a few details.

HAMLET: Your father's name?

ROMEO: I have three fathers, sir.

HAMLET: *(Dryly)* You must have had a wonderous mother.

But who the three?

ROMEO: The One in heaven, the one in flesh—

HAMLET: So far the same as I.

ROMEO: And lastly—

HAMLET: Yes?

ROMEO: The one who found me, gave me to the world,

by setting me upon ten thousand stages.

HAMLET: Dear brother! *(He embraces Romeo.)*

ROMEO: How say you, sir?

HAMLET: Will Shakespeare is the father of us both!

ROMEO: Could he have sent us here, at last to meet?

HAMLET: This mystery we should hasten to pursue.

ROMEO: At once, at once. But where's a bloody clue?

HAMLET: Well, here's for one. I died for love. And you?

ROMEO: The very fate was mine; I swear 'tis true.

And at the very thought I still could weep,

as if just now I'd found my love asleep.

HAMLET: We are condemned, like sinners, to our hell

for loving neither wisely *nor* too well.

Be of good cheer. P'raps heaven waits tomorrow.

From deeper streams, dear friend, doth spring my sorrow.

ROMEO: Despite the reenactments of my fate
　　　some hope cries madly that it's not too late.

HAMLET: *(He laughs.)* Ah, to be pained again by nothing more
　　　than youth's intrepid servant, ignorance,
　　　that, like an infant crying o'er spilt milk,
　　　assumes the present sorrow quite the worst
　　　and looks not to the future with its shocks
　　　that stand like shadows lined along our paths.

ROMEO: So let us talk of love, my friend, and see
　　　if somehow my heart's loss enriches thee.
　　　Yes, Love! We'll blend our stories into one
　　　to see what moral shines when we are done! *(Hamlet sighs deeply.)* Whose loss occasions such deep melancholy?

HAMLET: That of my father.

ROMEO: *(Sympathetically.)* Ah. You must have loved him much.

HAMLET: I loved him firstly as a father, Romeo,
　　　then as a man, and lastly as a hero.
　　　My heart's sustained three wounds.

ROMEO: You weep then at the loss of love.

HAMLET: Do not we all? We're taught to, from the cradle.

ROMEO: Quite so, we are. But these your thoughts on love
　　　strike echoes in my heart that hearing I
　　　must now relate to that the same disease
　　　from which I ache, am cured, to ache again.

HAMLET: Young friend, you'll learn our loves take many forms.
　　　There is a love of bodies' heady passion,
　　　that multitudes can satisfy, I swear;
　　　and there are other, higher, sweeter loves
　　　that on our hearts do make such great demands
　　　that only few, perchance 'twere even one,
　　　can properly accommodate. But know
　　　that there are loves for sisters, brothers, friends,
　　　for parents, cousins, strangers, dogs, and cats.
　　　You are a man, dear Romeo,
　　　which means you are a son,
　　　which means in turn
　　　a father drew you forth
　　　from out the timeless void
　　　of all the never-happened past.
　　　I weep for my lost father.

ROMEO: This shows a loving care in you, dear Hamlet
    but you should know your father lost a father,
    that father lost, lost his, and so
    it shall be until the general ending.
    Therefore, cease lament.
    It is a fault 'gainst heaven,
    a fault 'gainst nature, and in reason's
    common course most certain,
    none lives on earth but he is born to die.
HAMLET: Ah, Romeo, 'tis easy for you, now
    to lightly sweep my sharpest pains aside
    as, for that matter, I can nod at yours.
    But all the good Samaritans who've lived,
    could do no more than bind up fleshly wounds,
    assist with weights, bring water to our thirst,
    and set us on whatever proper roads
    our solitary fates might then decree.
    They cannot bleed for us, or weep for us,
    or die for us, but each must bear his own.
    Oh, that this too, too solid flesh would melt,
    thaw, and resolve itself into a dew,
    or that the everlasting had not
    fixed his cannon 'gainst self-slaughter.
    Within a month—married with my uncle:
    My father's brother! But no more like my father
    than I to Hercules. *(Woman enters.)*
    Within a month, ere yet the salt
    of most unrighteous tears had
    left the flushing in her galled eyes,
    she married. Why she, even she; oh
    God, a beast devoid of reason
    would have mourned longer.
    Frailty, thy name is woman!
WOMAN: One moment, sir. You claim we are inconstant?
HAMLET: Inconstant? Constantly!
WOMAN: Compared to what, I pray? To dogs, to clouds?
    To apes? To birds? To seasons in their turn?
ROMEO: To men, you silly woman!
WOMAN: So. Silly now, you say, as well as frail? *(Shakespeare peeks
    through window.)*
    That we are frail is all too clear, my prince.

The cause? That we are cursed with being human!
Humanity is frail, and vain and wild.
It must be so, as God the Father's child!
(Woman exits up staircase; Shakespeare closes window.)
ROMEO: Who was that?
HAMLET: Pay no mind.
ROMEO: What was your mother's crime?
HAMLET: Why, she would hang on him,
    as if increase of appetite had grown
    by what if fed on. Oh, wicked, wicked speed,
    to post with such dexterity to incestuous sheets.
    Ere yet those shoes were old
    with which she followed my poor father's body,
    like Niobe all tears. Married. With my uncle.
    Well it is not, nor can it come to good.
    But break my heart, for I must hold my tongue.
ROMEO: *(Wryly)* Your tongue lord Hamlet, seems most nimbly free.
    (To audience) Could man talk more? It seems not so to me.
    Perhaps, good friend, within the presence
    of those sinners you'd uncertainly accuse,
    tongueholding is suggested.
    But you see, I'm not a party to your tragedy.
    So freely speak, I pray you, for 'tis known
    that in the speaking out of wild emotion
    some strange release is thereby soon achieved,
    that doth make light the rumbling inner pressure
    that otherwise explodes our hearts and minds.
    At any rate, my friend, your father's gone.
    Nor all your tears or prayers can call him back.
    So after an appropriate sorrow's felt
    why not apply the energy of your emotion
    no more to that lost lonely realm, the Past,
    which, 'spite our hopes, we never shall improve,
    but rather to the other nearby kingdoms
    that in this world we have some hope to conquer?
HAMLET: Kingdoms?
ROMEO: I speak of Now and Future. There's the one
    we can be resolutely active in
    but as regards the other, we only plan.
    Yet, as I say, 'twere better so to do
    than waste our dreams and speculations on

the deeds that are solidified like crystal,
for all the endless time that lies behind
impervious to our saddest, fiercest hopes.

HAMLET: Though you say properly that past affairs
cannot be rearranged, we can withal
set out our future course the wisely more
if we're instructed by our past mistakes.
What *I* require, to balance despair, 's revenge!
The word itself is naught but angry sound
unless the past is carefully regarded.

ROMEO: Enough of this, good prince. Why come you here?

HAMLET: I have a duty that I must perform.
Though I can fully apprehend it not.
Yet moved I am in some mysterious way
that any man might tell of having felt.
(To audience) You witnesses in judgment here convened
can each remember, if you call it forth,
feeling compelled by fear, or by desire,
by avarice, or wish to avoid loss,
by hunger or by drowsiness, by weakness,
or any of a thousand shocks
that drive us on when otherwise we'd lie
like sullen cattle in the roadside's dust.
Just so, some odd foreknowledge of my fate
requires me here and now in this strange place,
anticipating I'll receive a message.

ROMEO: From whom, would it be mete to ask? *(Ghost appears dimly,
a forbidding spectre.)*

HAMLET: Your curiosity's resolved already, Romeo,
if you but turn and, stripping off the prejudice
that makes us blind to much, regard, I say,
the stately spectre who now comes our way.

ROMEO: *(He whirls and sees the Ghost.)* In truth, my Lord, it comes.
Though I do not believe in it
yet surely something here I sense.

HAMLET: Angels and ministers of grace, defend us!
Be thou a spirit of health, or goblin damned,
bring with thee airs from heaven or blasts from hell,
be thy intents wicked or charitable
thou comest in such a questionable shape
that I will speak to thee.

I'll call thee Hamlet, king, father, Royal Dane.
Oh, answer me, let me not burst in ignorance.
But tell why thy canonized bones
hearsed in death, have burst their cerements.
ROMEO: It beckons you, as though it had something
   to impart to you alone, but do not go with it.
HAMLET: It will not speak. Then I follow it.
ROMEO: What if it tempt you toward the flood, my Lord,
   or toward the dreadful summit of the cliff,
   that beetles o'er his base, into the sea
   and there assume some other horrible form
   which might deprive your sovereignty of reason
   and draw you into madness!
   Think of it!
HAMLET: Why, what should be the fear?
   I do not set my life at a pin's fee.
   And for my soul, what can it do to that,
   being a thing immortal, as itself?
GHOST: Mark me.
HAMLET: I will.
GHOST: I am thy father's spirit, doomed for a time
   to walk the night, and all the day,
   confined to flaming fire
   till the foul crimes done in my days of nature
   are burnt and purged away.
HAMLET: Alas, poor ghost, from purgatory come.
GHOST: Nay, pity me not, but to my unfolding
   lend thy listening ear. But that I am forbid
   to tell the secrets of my prison house
   I would a tale unfold whose lightest word
   would harrow up thy soul, freeze thy young blood,
   make thy two eyes like stars that start from their spheres,
   thy knotted and combine'd locks to part
   and each particular hair to stand on end
   like quills upon the fretful porcupine.
   But this eternal blazon must not be
   to ears of flesh and blood.
   Hamlet, if ever thou didst thy dear father love—
HAMLET: Oh, God.
GHOST: Revenge his foul and most unnatural murder.
HAMLET: Murder?

GHOST: Yea, murder in the highest degree
     as in the least 'tis bad.
     But mine most foul, beastly, and unnatural.
     A serpent stung me. He that did sting
     thy father's heart, now wears his crown.
HAMLET: Oh, my prophetic soul. My uncle.
GHOST: Aye, that adulterous beast won to his will with gifts—
     oh, wicked will, and gifts, that have the power
     so to seduce thy most seeming virtuous queen.
HAMLET: Oh, God.
GHOST: If thou hast nature in thee, bear it not.
     But howsoever let not thy heart
     conspire against thy mother ought. Leave her to heaven.
     And to the burden that her conscience bears.
     (The Ghost withdraws.)
ROMEO: God's wounds! What's to become of you?
HAMLET: *(Still shaken)* Once more to walk the old accustomed path,
     an instrument of vengeance. Oh cursed spite
     that I was born to set it right.
ROMEO: I say again:
     You cannot change the past, and never ought
     To venture out on orders from thin air.
HAMLET: *(Furiously)* Thin air? You doubt?
ROMEO: I do.
     Consider, friend, I pray, that we have both
     been sore deceived, that what you took as real
     was built not of true spirit but of dreams,
     that whose firm voice you heard, or thought you heard,
     came truly not from Death's unknown domain
     but from the echous cavern of your mind
     wherein wild giants rage. You know their names.
HAMLET: I do?
ROMEO: Yes. Jealousy and mad Desire.
     Consider what foul imaginings result
     when monstrous creatures such as these convene,
     each guided by none other than itself
     and each unused to reprimand or rule.
     It is the kingdom of pure wintry chaos;
     it lures us to none other than our death
     if we're not guided by another sense
     superior and lighted by the virtues.

HAMLET: How now? You've seen, you've heard, and still you doubt?

ROMEO: I do indeed, my prince. But doubt is not
    the same as flat denial. I heard, as did
    these witnesses, and yet we surely know
    what strange contagions touch our weakly minds
    that one man's madness may affect another.
    The hypnotists make use of this, conspiring
    with weaknesses that grow in us from birth
    to make us certain that the moon's the sun,
    that snow is hot, or fire as cold as ice.
    (He laughs.) I saw a man once freely hypnotized
    who took a Spanish onion in his hand,
    snapped an enormous portion with his jaws,
    he having been assured it was the sweetest,
    juiciest apple he had e'er enjoyed.
    If it be so, then how can we be sure
    that I have done no more than share your visions?

HAMLET: Well, something in me's sure if you are not.

ROMEO: If only there were others who could witness,
    adjudicate, decide the issue for us. *(Woman enters unobtrusively.)*

HAMLET: Would it were so, but to bring in a third
    would do no more than far extrapolate
    that doubt which saps the iron from our wills.
    I'd say his judgment good if it conformed
    to my own prejudice; and if't did not
    I would as soon declare him enemy.
    (He takes his sword in hand.)

WOMAN: You would, you silly man. *(Laughs.)* Circumstance
    Could change your course as quickly as a blink.

HAMLET: Not so!

WOMAN: Ten thousand times just so! We need but add
    a third with stronger steel than your own.
    You apprehend him stronger, braver, tall!
    Thus cowardice makes conscience for us all!
    (The Woman makes her conjuring gesture.)

OTHELLO: *(He enters, stares fiercely at Hamlet and his weapon, then
    draws his own.)* Your pleasure, sir?

HAMLET: *(He wavers momentarily, then sheaths his blade.)* Peace, good
    soldier.

OTHELLO: A pleasure all too rare in my experience.

WOMAN: "He who fights and runs away lives to fight another day."
  The basic principle of guerilla warfare.
HAMLET: *(Somewhat aggrieved by her sarcasm.)* Discretion is the better
  part of valor.
ROMEO: Woman, would you stir one 'gainst the other?
  We seek to know how we may love our brother.
WOMAN: Don't let me stop you. Pray proceed. *(Woman catches
  Shakespeare peeking through window, laughs, withdraws to the
  fireplace.)*
OTHELLO: Othello, called the Moor of Venice.
  (He and Romeo clasp forearms in greeting.)
ROMEO: Greetings, General. Your servant, Romeo.
  This man is Hamlet, Prince of Denmark.
OTHELLO: *(He bows respectfully.)* Your Highness.
HAMLET: We do not stand on ceremony here, good soldier.
OTHELLO: You know me?
HAMLET: *(He nods.)* But only insofar as you know me. Enough of
  that. You're just in time to judge.
OTHELLO: Of what, my Lord?
HAMLET: Of whether there be ghosts or no and if
  there are then whether I've been visited
  by my late father.
OTHELLO: And if you have?
HAMLET: Why then I must prepare my soul for vengeance.
OTHELLO: I never knew one not prepared, my Lord.
  It might be thought revenge was soldiers' business.
  But oft' a man will shoulder us aside
  and do the job himself.
  Your end, I fear, will be the very same
  whether spirits from the grave return or not.
ROMEO: How came you to acquire such wisdom, soldier?
OTHELLO: It grows from my disinterestedness.
  Having no stake in this good man's predicament
  I may assume a sage neutrality.
HAMLET: As regards your own predicament?
OTHELLO: *(He smiles.)* I beg your counsel, sir, and yours.
HAMLET: We had begun a discourse on sweet love.
OTHELLO: Continue.
HAMLET: But only if you'll join. You know of it?
OTHELLO: I died of it.
ROMEO: Your story, pray.

OTHELLO: Romeo and Hamlet, I'm rich now
  with that poor hindsight which, if 'twere seen before,
  would have reversed my fate.
HAMLET: And yet, dark Moor, a happy ending to your tale
  might render us less interested, I fear.
ROMEO: In all events, what's done is done.
  There's no denying there's a market for extremes
  and if we'll not have one, then haste the other.
  I spoke of thwarted young romantic love;
  brave Hamlet here of love in other guise.
HAMLET: Yes, love of father.
ROMEO: Really? I saw it more as love of mother.
  That love which men first count a glowing virtue
  but if it not diminish through the years
  leads to vile guilts but poorly understood.
HAMLET: If anything is richly understood.
  And watch that talk about my mother, friend.
ROMEO: I'll say whatever I damned please.
HAMLET: Not in my presence, by God!
OTHELLO: Gentlemen!
HAMLET: He's no gentleman.
ROMEO: *(He lunges at Hamlet. Othello stops him.)* He thinks he's placed
  so high and mighty!
  My problems were a good deal worse than yours.
HAMLET: Oh, you think so?! You think it's easy
  being Hamlet?
ROMEO: I fail to see the difficulty.
HAMLET: All right, then you be Hamlet for awhile.
ROMEO: All right, and you be Romeo, if you think you're man enough!
HAMLET: You bastard! *(He exchanges part of his costume with Romeo.)*
  There! Now I am Romeo.
ROMEO: And I am Hamlet! *(From this point the
  two actors switch parts.)*
WOMAN: And I am bored! *(She exits.)*
OTHELLO: Now that that's settled, gentlemen, may I continue?
HAMLET: Most certainly.
  Before this jackanapes erupts again.
  Pray, share with us your story.
  On which aspect of love will you address us?
OTHELLO: I bring a tale of jealousy, that sorrowed segment
  of a lovely whole, that bitter dripping

of the sweetest fruit,
that poison from a medicine distilled.

HAMLET: We've all made some mistake. Pray, what was yours?

OTHELLO: That I was such a deadly judge of character
I knew not friend from foe, each the other.
My friend, one Michael Cassio, a Florentine,
a mathematician and an officer,
who held naught but the warmest regard for me,
and innocent affection for my wife;
but he I thought my friend, the vile Iago,
ah, let him be instructive to all men,
the warning signal being flattery.
When 'ere it's heard be on thy guard, good friends,
for though there moments be when it's sincere
some kinds of compliments are less than dear.

ROMEO: And what the soil from which your sorrows grew?

OTHELLO: From that of Venice, which you may well know.
I mightily by daybreak had destroyed the Turk,
had swept the seas of his foul bark and threat
(albeit with some help from savage nature)
and so deserved Venetian honors well,
And—double triumph—took the fairest prize
the city could bestow, Desdemona, the daughter of Brabantio.
Had I but known that at the drama's start
Iago profaned what he claimed to bless
by telling good Brabantio his daughter
and your servant were abed.

ROMEO: I'll wager you were.

OTHELLO: *(He smiles.)* Iago warned me that Brabantio was much
beloved
and had in his effect a voice potential
as double as the Duke's. He would divorce us
or put upon us what restrain or grievance
the law with all its might to enforce on
would give him cable.

ROMEO: You didn't let him get away with that, I hope.

OTHELLO: I did not. "Let him do his spite,"
I cried. My services which I have done the Signorie
could out-tongue his complaints.
My troth was justified by Senators,
who put the interests of the city at the fore.

At which Brabantio, her father, pardoned me,
yet supposed I'd stolen Desdemona
by drugs or medicines, bought of montebanks,
by witchcraft, or by magic of my own.
HAMLET: And had you so?
OTHELLO: 'Twas never thus. I spoke my heart:
"Most potent, grave, and reverend *signores,*
my very noble and approved good masters,
that I have taken away this old man's daughter
it is most true, true I have married her.
The very head and front of my offending, hath this extent.
No more. Rude am I in my speech
and little blessed with the soft phrase of peace
for, since these arms of mine had seven years pith
till now, some nine moons wasted, they have used
their dearest action in the tented field.
And little of this great world can I speak
more than pertains to feats of broil and battle
and therefore little shall I grace my cause
in speaking for myself. Yet, by your gracious patience
I will a round, unvarnished tale deliver
of my whole course of love. What drugs, what charms,
what conjuration, and what mighty magic
(for such proceeding I am charged withall)
I won his daughter. I do beseech you
send for the lady to the Sagitary,
and let her speak of me before her father.
If you do find me foul in her report
that trust the office I do hold of you,
not only take away, but let your sentence
even fall upon my life.
Her father loved me, oft invited me,
still questioned me the story of my life.
From year to year: the battles, sieges, fortune,
that I have passed.
I ran it through, even from my boyish days
to the very moment when he bade me tell it,
wherein I spake of most disatrous chances,
of moving accidents by flood and field,
of hair-bredth 'scapes in the imminent deadly breech,
of being taken by the insolent foe

and sold to slavery, of my redemption thence,
and portance in my travel's history
wherein antres vast and deserts idle,
rough quarries, rocks, and hills,
whose heads touch heaven,
it was my hint to speak. Such was process
and of the cannibals that each other eat.
These things to hear would Desdemona seriously incline
but still the house affairs would call her hence
whichever, as she would with haste dispatch,
she'd come again and with a greedy ear
devour up my discourse. . . .
My story being done,
she gave me for my pains a world of sighs.
She swore in faith 'twas strange, 'twas passing strange,
'twas pitiful, 'twas wondrous pitiful.
She wished she had not heard it, yet she wished
heaven had made her such a man. She thanked me
and bade me, if I had a friend that loved her,
I should but teach him how to tell my story
and that would woo her."

HAMLET: Upon this hint you spoke?

OTHELLO: Yes. She loved me for the dangers I had passed
and I loved her that she did pity them.
This only is the witchcraft I had used.

ROMEO: But whence came evil to this lovely scene?

HAMLET: He's already answered that, Romeo.
You're not paying attention.

ROMEO: I'm beginning to think I should pay closer attention to *you*.

HAMLET: Do so. You might learn something.

OTHELLO: Gentlemen, just a moment ago you were talking about
brotherly love.

ROMEO: You're right, Othello. I'm sorry.
I'm not myself this evening.
(He does a take.) But of course I'm not.

HAMLET: Shall we?

ROMEO: Certainly. *(They exchange clothing and recover their original
identities.)*

HAMLET: Now, where were we?

OTHELLO: I was explaining, 'twas Iago. He the serpent
who crept into our paradise to take

the dazzling fruit of wonderment and doubt
to tempt me with and so to turn me out.

HAMLET: Could he not leave the well enough alone?

ROMEO: Had he some jealousy of love itself?

OTHELLO: Aye, you've said it. He claimed he'd never known a man
that knew precisely how to love himself.
He little thought of love, nor any virtue.
'Twas only in ourselves he said, that we are thus and thus,
our bodies are our gardens to the which—

IAGO: *(Enters, taking over.)* Our wills are gardeners. So if we will
plant nettles or sow lettuce,
to have it sterile with idleness
or manured with industry, the power and
corrigible authority lies in our wills.
If the balance of our lives had not one scale of reason
to poise another of sensuality
the blood and baseness of our natures
would conduct us to the most preposterous conclusions.
But we have reason to cool our raging emotions,
our carnal stings, our strong unbitted lusts.

OTHELLO: *(Still unaware of Iago)* Therefore, he said, what we call love's
no more than lust of blood.
He placed more trust in money-in-the-purse,
which time could only slowly then consume,
than in strong loves, which he supposed were short.
I see, though all too late, that fruits of love to him
were grapes that, falling short of,
he did mark as sour.

ROMEO: Was there no happiness at all for you?

OTHELLO: Yes, for a while I basked in beauty.
It gave me wonder great as my content
to see her oft' before me.
Oh, my soul's joy
if after every tempest came such calms.
May strong winds blow, till they've awakened death
and let the laboring bark climb hills of seas
Olympus-high, and duck again as low
as hell's from heaven. If it were then to die
'twere then to be most happy.

ROMEO: You looked about the world and saw but beauty.

OTHELLO: *(He nods.)* "Come, let us to the castle, friends," I called.

"News, friends, our wars are done,
the Turks are drowned."
Iago, that foul traitor, quick perceived
the thunderous momentum of my love
could serve to throw my soul off-balance,
as Orientals so employ the thrust
of foes to overturn them on the charge.
He noised about that Cassio loved her
which in a sense he did, but as a friend.
He next related how my blessed wife
returned that favor, as indeed she should.
And then, by sly exaggeration of the truth,
began to build a vile and ugly structure.
"Now I do love her, too,"
he claimed apart.

IAGO: *(From balcony)* Not out of absolute lust,
but partly led to diet my revenge
that I do think the lusty Moor
hath leaped into my seat, the thought whereof
doth—like a poisonous mineral—gnaw my inwards.
And nothing can or shall content my soul
till I am evened with him, wife for wife.

OTHELLO: All this he said, though then I knew it not.

IAGO: Or failing so, yet that I put the Moor at least
into a jealousy so strong
that judgment cannot cure. Which thing to do,
I'll have our Michael Cassio on the hip,
abuse him to the Moor, in the rank garb,
make the Moor thank me, love me, and reward me
for making him egregiously an ass.

ROMEO: But if a man speaks naught but lies, my Lord,
was not some faint suspicion 'ere aroused?

OTHELLO: Had it been so, young friend, I would indeed
have questioned much of what the villain said.

HAMLET: *(To Romeo)* But know you not the Devil truly speaks
a thousand times, that we'll believe one lie?

OTHELLO: Some of the man's advice was sound, you see.
He told me, for example, that good name
in man or woman was the jewel of spirit.

IAGO: Who steals my purse steals trash,
'tis something, nothing. 'Twas mine, 'tis his.

And had been slave to thousands.
But he that filches from me my good name
robs me of that which not enriches him
and makes me poor indeed.

OTHELLO: By heaven, I'll know your thoughts.

IAGO: You cannot, if my heart were in your hand;
nor shall not whilst 'tis in *my* custody.

OTHELLO: Ha!

IAGO: O, beware, my Lord, of jealousy!
It is the green-eyed monster, which doth mock
the sorry meat it feeds on. That cuckold lives in bliss
who, certain of his fate, loves not his wronger;
but oh, what damn'ed minutes tells he o'er
who dotes, yet doubts—suspects, yet fondly loves!
Good heaven, the souls of all my tribe defend
from jealousy!

OTHELLO: Avaunt, begone. Thou has set me on the rack.
I swear, 'tis better to be much abused
than but to know it a little.
What sense had I in her stol'n hours of lust?
I saw't not, thought it not, it harmed not me.
I slept the next night well, fed well, was free and merry.
I found not Cassio's kisses on her lips.
He that is robbed, not wanting what is stolen,
let him not know it, he's not robbed at all.
I had been happy, if the general camp,
pioneers and all, had tasted her sweet body,
so I had nothing known. Oh, now forever
farewell the tranquil mind, farewell content,
fairwell the plume'd troops, and the big wars
that make ambition virtue! Ah, farewell.
Farewell the neighing steed and the shrill trumpet,
the spirit-stirring drum, th' ear-piercing fife,
the royal banner, and all quality,
pride, pomp, and circumstance of glorious war.
And oh, you mortal engines, whose rude throats
the immortal Jove's dread clamor counterfeit,
farewell. Othello's occupation's gone. *(Throws sword down.)*
'Twas thus I spoke and thus I deeply felt.
At last to such a pitch of jealous rage
I rose—or is it fell?—that sweet revenge

was all I wanted, ordered Cassio's death
and could not rest until I saw his blood.
And then, most vile of all, I snarled and snapped
an angry wolf at that dear child's throat.

HAMLET: Did not your love's denials, when at last
you false accused her, give you pause?

OTHELLO: *(He sighs, speaking chiefly to himself.)* There is a satisfaction
vile in evil
that, though it turns on us and does us pain,
we yet persist. Ah, most of what we say
the world is doing to us, we are doing
to ourselves. I told my heaven's angel
that she was false as hell and wept the tears of madness.

HAMLET: I wonder if such deeds required Iago,
or are we equal to the fearful task
of ordering our dismantlement ourselves?
But we shall understand Iago not
if he is but our scapegoat.
There must be something hidden in our souls
that wants to hear the worst.

ROMEO: Not in my case!
Death separated me from love
but by a gross mistake.

OTHELLO: My suffering far exceeds your own, good Romeo,
for to my sense of loss there's added guilt
and each compounds the other a thousandfold.

WOMAN: *(As Desdemona, she suddenly materializes from out of darkness and approaches Othello.)* Does it, indeed, my love?

OTHELLO: Desdemona!

WOMAN: Then, pray do tell
why you could not escape your separate hell,
why, in your struggle between love and hate,
you learned which one was weak and which was great.
Love, it would seem, is a fair-weather friend
that in the spring vows it will never end
but that in winter when the fury comes,
is shocked, is shaken, and at last succumbs.
At least it's so with love of mortal men
who first would give a kingdom for a touch.
We women know love's something else again.
We love the more expecting half as much.

OTHELLO: *(He holds the Woman by the throat, first tenderly, then in violence.)* Sweet soul, take heed of perjury.

Thou art on thy deathbed.
Therefore confess thee freely of thy sin
for to deny each article with oath
cannot remove nor choke the strong conception
that I do groan withal. Thou art to die!
By heaven, I saw my handkerchief in his hand!
Oh, perjured woman, thou dost stone my heart
and makes me call what I intend to do
a murder, which I thought a sacrifice. *(Desdemona is dead by his hand. Very tenderly he lowers her body to the stairs.)*

HAMLET: *(Gently)* And justice found you at the end, Othello?
Pray say it did; I needs must think it so.

OTHELLO: Yes. Mine the just desserts of infamy.
And yet, though fool I was, murderer, knave,
I did my state some service and they knew it.
No more of that. I pray you, in your letters
when you shall these unlucky deeds relate
speak of me as I am. Nothing extenuate
nor set down aught in malice. Then you must speak
of one that loved not wisely but too well;
of one not easily jealous, but being
perplexed in the extreme. Of one who's hand
like the base Indian, who threw a pearl away
richer than all his tribe, of one whose subdued eyes
albeit unused to the melting mood
drop tears as fast as the Arabian trees
their medicinable gum. This set you down,
and say besides that in Aleppo once,
where a malignant and a turbaned Turk
beat a Venetian and traduced the state,
I took by the throat the circumsized dog
and smote him, as at my dire end, I smote myself.
So gentlemen, because one villain lied
my dignity, my love, myself all died.

STEVE: *(Enters. Characters are frozen in place.)* Well, this has been a strange experience, I am sure you'll agree. I've been looking for Shakespeare himself, but without success.

In any event, we've seen, this evening, some of the ways in which Shakespeare dealt with the theme of love. It's been interesting enough, needless to say, but I had hoped to put questions to the playwright directly, rather than just make inferences about his views on love from the fates and lines he devised for his characters.

We're sorry to leave things so up in the air, but I'll tell you what. Why don't you join us again next time, for part two of our discussion? We hope Shakespeare will return. If he does we'll ask him about the most beautiful love poems ever written, his famous sonnets. No doubt his answers will be instructive.

Thank you, and good night.

SHOW # 18

William Shakespeare
(HARRIS YULIN)

Woman
(JAYNE MEADOWS)

Hamlet
(ANTHONY COSTELLO)

Othello
(WILLIAM MARSHALL)

Romeo
(CHARLES LANYER)

Welcome again to Meeting of Minds. Tonight we present part two
of a special dramatic presentation titled "Shakespeare on Love."

If you were with us last time, you will recall that our guests
were William Shakespeare, Prince Hamlet of Denmark, Romeo
Montague of Verona, Othello, the Moor of Venice, and a remarkable creature known as *Woman.* And now once again your host. . .
Steve Allen.

STEVE: Thank you and good evening. Well, if you were with us last
time you'll know that the *first* of our pair of programs with William
Shakespeare turned out to be—uh—unusual. For one thing, the
three chief guests who showed up to discuss Shakespeare's views
on the subject of love turned out to be not important personages
from history—as is usually the case here—but three imaginary
characters—Hamlet, Romeo, and Othello.

But perhaps the most remarkable development was the intrusion
into our regular format of an uninvited guest who chose to refer
to herself simply as Woman. One moment she was the mysterious
Dark Lady of the Sonnets, at another Desdemona.

My own inclinations are nothing if not experimental, so I didn't
particulary object to the fact that she blithely disregarded the general rules of our game. But I think most of us were taken aback
by her attitude toward Shakespeare. We regard him as history's
greatest poet and dramatist. She, on the other hand, looked at
him—now that I come to think of it—in a way that many people
who know heroic figures personally, and intimately, regard them,
which is to say with less than customary respect.

In any event it was most interesting to hear Hamlet tell of his
love for his father. Or, as Romeo thought the situation might be
construed, love for his mother. The two not being mutually exclu-
sive, of course.

Romeo made passing references to his passionate, romantic love
for the beautiful Juliet, and I assume he'll be adding further details
this evening.

As for Othello, he gave us quite a complete resumé of his tragic
love-relationship with Desdemona, which ended—as you know—
with his killing her in a fit of jealous rage.

Speaking personally, I've prepared no interview questions for our
guests, as I ordinarily do—I usually have my notes, as you know—
except for William Shakespeare himself. But, unfortunately, last
time he panicked when the Dark Lady of the Sonnets—or *whoever*
the heck she was—burst in, and—uh—he ran off. I have the idea,

however, that if only because we *do* expect another visit by three
of his most famous creatures, he might well be lurking about the
premises. Perhaps we might even be fortunate enough to entice
him back to our stage to continue sharing with us his views on
the subject of that which, it is said, makes the world go round.
The thoughts of Shakespeare on love would certainly be of profound interest to us all, I'm sure. But I was—

WOMAN: *(She flings open the double-doors, and gestures to attract
Steve's attention.)* Sir!

STEVE: Huh!

WOMAN: Sir. Would you come here, please, quickly!

STEVE: Yes. *(To audience.)* Excuse me, I'm afraid we're in trouble.
Yes? *(He hurries off through the double-doors, which close behind
him.) (Offstage)* Where are you?

WOMAN: *(She magically appears now on the other side of the stage,
smiling, self-satisfied.)* Now that *he's* out of the way—
(She addresses the audience.) I've been concerned to demonstrate,
my friends
that Shakespeare's gifts were purely for the *writing,*
Not for *living.*
If this bespectacled nonentity
who called him here imagined for a minute
Will would solve the mysteries of love,
why, it's really quite absurd.
Now, let me see. Ah, yes. I'd brought you
Will's most famous lovers: Othello, Hamlet, Romeo.
They've much to learn.
Let's see if they can do it. *(She repeats her magical gesture, three
times. At each wave of her hand a figure appears. For a moment
they stand stiffly, almost as statuary. Then, with another gesture,
she brings them to life.)*
(To audience.) I'd no idea, my friends, a week ago
when first we met, what that one hour would show.
That, as for love, these three as well could sit
and hear each one of you discourse on it.
You've loved as much, no doubt, or so I trust,
seen love you'd wish survive dissolve to dust,
seen other loves scarce worthy of the name
burst wild and unexpectedly aflame.
If all the world's a stage, as Will has said,
then each of *you* no doubt, tucked in his head

has some tempestuous story you'd convey
if only you, not us, were in this play.

HAMLET: Loquacious woman, would you talk all night?

WOMAN: Well, that depends, my Lord. Perhaps I might.

HAMLET: This shrew requires taming, does she not?

WOMAN: You could not do it, sir, with what you've got.
(She exits.)

OTHELLO: *(He laughs.)* No shrew was ever tamed but on the stage.
Love's far too sweet to ever conquer rage.

HAMLET: We bear a heavy burden from our master.

OTHELLO: But now, young friend, your story I'd hear more,
Of Juliet, whom you learned so to adore.

HAMLET: Yes.

ROMEO: I tell you first of long and bloody feud
which, sweeping up the individual,
doth give him lesser mastery of his fate,
than wind-tossed leaves may claim before a storm.

HAMLET: And what strong fortress, pray, was in your time
the city of Verona raised against?

ROMEO: No other city then, m'Lord. The war
of which I speak was that between two clans,
the Capulets and Montagues. 'Twas true
what said some other citizens thereby:
Down with Capulets, down with the Montagues,
for they had given Verona much abuse.
The case was well put by my Prince Escalus
who called rebellious subjects enemies to peace.
"What ho," he said to both, "you men, you beasts
that quench the fire of your pernicious rage
with purple fountains issuing from your veins.
On pain of torture, from those bloody hands
throw your mistempered weapons to the ground
and hear the sentence of your move'd Prince.
If ever you disturb our streets again
your lives shall pay the forfeit of the peace."

HAMLET: And took you part in this unseemly strife?

ROMEO: As far as willing, no. I kept apart
and many a morning had I then been seen
with tears augmenting the fresh morning's dew
adding to more clouds with my deep sighs.
But all so soon as the all-cheering sun

did in the farthest East begin to draw
the shady curtains from Aurora's bed,
away from light I stole, perplexed in mind,
and private in my chamber penned myself,
shut up my windows, locked fair daylight out,
and made myself an artificial night.

HAMLET: And love brought you to such a low estate?

ROMEO: Indeed, my Lord. I suffered as from hate,
that fearful opposite which must bring suffering,
for yet the choirs of love can dirges sing.

OTHELLO: But you were handsome, Romeo, and young.
Pray, tell from whence your sorrows sprung.
Was she you loved a prisoner, or worse,
or dead, hidden underneath a curse?
Or was she very young, a child like yourself?

ROMEO: A child, and an angel, and an elf.
She had not seen the change of fourteen years
and hers were then only the simplest fears.
Two years more were to wither in their pride
'ere she was thought prepared to be a bride.
The youth Count Paris was her father's choice
to teach her what it is makes wives rejoice.
One night he held an old accustomed feast,
invited guests from north, south, west, and east,
told Paris then that to behold that night
earth-treading stars did make dark heaven light.
My friend Mercutio and I did plan
to tend the festive board in some disguise,
each to pretend to be some other man.

HAMLET: Did you spy her with whom your fate was cast?

ROMEO: Scarce had I entered than she came to sight, *(Woman appears,*
   radiant, as Juliet, pantomimes conversation with another player.)
she who taught flaming torches to burn bright.
It seemed she hung upon the cheek of night
as a rich jewel in an Ethiop's ear,
beauty too rich for use, for earth too dear.
I stared, I smiled, wild music filled my head,
and to my fairest Juliet I said,
"If I profane with my unworthiest hand
this holy shrine, the gentle fine is this,

my lips two blushing pilgrims ready stand
to smooth that rough touch with a tender kiss."
WOMAN: Good pilgrim, you do wrong your hand too much
which mannerly devotion shows in this,
for saints have hands that pilgrims' hands do touch
And palm-to-palm is holy palmers' kiss.
(Darkness obscures Juliet, who withdraws.)
ROMEO: *(He turns back to his companions.)* 'Twas only then I learned
her Capulet.
HAMLET: No!
ROMEO: *(He nods.)* What strange account, my life in my foe's debt.
The light, the dance, the sport were at the best
but I so feared the more was my unrest.
I later learned that as I left the room
fair Juliet's ecstasy was plunged to gloom.
She learned my name was Montague and felt
her happy confidence begin to melt.
Her only love sprung from her only hate,
too early seen, unknown, and known too late.
OTHELLO: You saw her not again?
ROMEO: Oh, yes, I did.
I was determined to review that face,
to draw a blessing from that saintly grace.
My friends saw humor that I shyly mooned.
He jests at scars that never felt a wound.

But soft, what light through yonder window breaks?
It is the East, and Juliet is the sun.
Arise, fair sun, and kill the envious moon
who is already sick and pale with grief
that thou, her maid, are far more fair than she.
Be not her maid since she is envious.
Her vestal livery is but sick and green,
and none but fools do wear it. Cast it off.
(Woman as Juliet appears on staircase.)
It is my lady, oh, it is my love.
Oh, that she knew she were.
She speaks, yet she says nothing. What of that?
Her eye discourses. I will answer it.
I am too bold. 'Tis not to me she speaks.
Two of the fairest stars in all the heavens,

having some business, do entreat her eyes
to twinkle in their spheres till they return.
What if her eyes were there? They in her head,
the brightness of her cheek would shame those stars
as daylight doth a lamp. Her eyes in heaven
would through the airy regions stream so bright
that birds would sing and think it were not right.
See how she leans her cheek upon her hand.
Oh, that I were a glove upon that hand,
that I might touch that cheek.

WOMAN: Ay, me.

ROMEO: She speaks. Oh, speak again, bright angel, for thou art
as glorious to this night being o'er my head
as is a winged messenger of heaven
onto the white upturned wondering eyes
of mortals who fall back to gaze on him
when he bestrides the lazy pacing clouds
and sails upon the bosom of the air.

WOMAN: Oh, Romeo, Romeo, wherefore art thou Romeo?
Deny thy father and *refuse* thy name,
Or, if thou wilt not, be but sworn my love
and I'll no longer be a Capulet.
What's in a name? That which we call a rose
by any other name would smell as sweet.
So Romeo would, were he not Romeo called,
retain that dear perfection which he owes
without that title. Romeo, doff thy name
and for thy name, which is no part of thee,
take all myself.

ROMEO: Lady, by yonder blessed moon I—

HAMLET: Wait a minute! Wait a minute! That's not the right approach
at all.

WOMAN: What?

HAMLET: He's doing it all wrong.

ROMEO: You think that you'd be any better?

HAMLET: Of course.

ROMEO: I'm getting pretty sick of this!

HAMLET: I was getting sick *watching* it!

OTHELLO: Gentlemen, I pray you. Cease this bickering.

WOMAN: Yes, get on with it! Where were we?

OTHELLO: Doff thy name—and so forth—

WOMAN: Thank you.

OTHELLO: It's nothing.

WOMAN: Oh, Romeo, doff thy name
and for thy name, which is no part of thee
take all myself.

ROMEO: By yonder blessed moon—

HAMLET: Still, names do ring bells in us.
They're not as empty as Juliet supposes.
I knew a merchant once in Amsterdam. Try Ginsburg,
making such alterations as seem wise.

WOMAN: Oh, Ginsburg, Ginsburg, wherefore art thou Ginsburg?
Deny thy father and refuse thy name.

HAMLET: My father once, he said, did smite
a sledder Pollack on the ice.
So, try—Woznowski.

WOMAN: Oh, Woznowski, Woznowski, Why art thou Woznowski?

OTHELLO: Hamlet, you've a disrespectful spirit
that borders now on madness.

HAMLET: Madness with some method in it, soldier.
(To Romeo) Your pardon, sir.

ROMEO: *(Touchily)* If no offense intended, none inferred.
In any case she called me Love and I was new baptized.
From then the name Romeo I never prized.
Lady—I cried—by yonder blessed moon I swear
that tips with silver all these fruit-tree tops.
At that she paled and bid me change my vow.
I mind her admonition even now:

WOMAN: Oh, swear not by the moon, the inconstant moon
that monthly changes in her circled orb,
lest that thy love prove likewise variable.
Or, if thou wilt, swear by thy gracious self,
which is the god of my idolatry,
and I'll believe thee.

ROMEO: We swore our love a thousand ways that night
and then at last she vanished from my sight. *(Juliet is obscured by darkness.)* Love goes toward love as schoolboys from their books
but love from love, toward school with heavy looks.
Good night, she said, then breathed good night again.
For which I was the happiest of men.

"Parting," she said to me, "is such sweet sorrow,
that I shall say good night 'till it be morrow."

OTHELLO: Did you make haste to make the lady yours?

ROMEO: I did. Told Friar Lawrence we would wed,
that, rath'r than live without her, I'd be dead.

HAMLET: Why then, what went wrong with the plans you built?

ROMEO: What *didn't?* Help us all, much blood was spilt.
Rude Tybalt of the Capulets did tempt
me to forget the dreams I'd dreamt.
He threatened my good friend Mercutio,
to tell him where he might find Romeo.

OTHELLO: And these calm words but drove your friend to rage?

ROMEO: *(He withdraws his rapier.)* Yes. He commanded Tybalt to take
stage.
"Tybalt, thou rat-catcher," cried he, "willst walk?
If coward thou not be, let thy blade talk!"
Mercutio of death-knells heard the sound.
At first I thought him hurt but lightly, then
I soon perceived he would not rise again.
"But courage, man"—I said—"th' hurt can't be
beyond the courage of your own capacity."
"No," he said. His sarcasm truly hurt,
as bravely he lay dying in the dirt.
" 'Tis not so deep, this wound, as garden well
nor quite so wide as church-door, but by hell
it is enough. 'Twill serve. Seek me tomorrow
and you shall find the reason mourners sorrow.
A plague on both your houses," then he said,
and, rightly blaming me, he fell back dead.
I rose then in my rage and Tybalt slew,
and where there'd been one dead,
there now lay two.

HAMLET: So then where previously there'd been hate
between your houses now 'twas twice as great.

ROMEO: *(He nods.)* And our good Prince did sentence to exile
the fool who stands before you all this while.

HAMLET: Enough, my friend. Withhold your tale's conclusion
for, knowing how our master weaves confusion
with woof of history, warp of its truth,
I sense death's ending to this tale of youth.

ROMEO: Would that I could deny it. Strange, good friends,

how Master Will contrived such deadly ends
for us who never did him slighest harm.
OTHELLO: Against a devil any man might arm.
   But doth it not seem, sir, surpassing odd
   that we'd require protection from our god?
HAMLET: *(He laughs.)* You've never read the Scriptures? *(Othello laughs heartily.)*
   I must observe, Othello,
   you are a stout companion and good fellow.
OTHELLO: And why, dear Hamlet, should our mood be other?
   Our father was the same, so we are brother.
   (He puts his arms around the other two men's shoulders.)
   We three are one, my friends. But now I fear
   'tis time to seek the reason we are here.
ROMEO: What think you?
HAMLET: What gift of prophecy instructs you now?
OTHELLO: Why, none at all, my Lord. We've an appointment.
HAMLET: Simple as that?
OTHELLO: I feel so.
HAMLET: And to what end, I pray?
OTHELLO: The very one we've shown, to speak of love. To share our
   knowledge and experience.
HAMLET: Dear friends, I've just now realized
   wherein lies love's most chief distinction.
ROMEO: Which is?
HAMLET: That all that we're long trained in we become
   most expert at save this. Why, let a man do
   husbandry, or music, farming, war,
   and he becomes a veteran and a sage.
   But love, which he drinks in with mother's milk,
   knows as an infant, schoolboy, brawling youth,
   he's faulty at till death, and even at best
   would never boast he's mastered such an art.
   And yet—*(A feeling strikes him.)* Wait!
ROMEO: What is it?
HAMLET: I have a sense of imminence this night,
   almost religious. There is news to come.
ROMEO: Our souls are in deep dark, desiring light:
   Receiving gift of tongues of else struck dumb.
OTHELLO: Look! *(He points to the back of the theatre.)*
WOMAN: One moment, gentlemen. *(She gestures and the three do a*

"freeze-frame" pose. She addresses a particular man in the audience.)
    You, sir, having heard these masters three
    reveal their secret souls to thee and me,
    feel you more gifted at the loving arts
    or still as puzzled by this game of hearts?
    Well, if you can but wait a moment more
    there's one who would address you from this floor.
    He's here, and by the mothers who have borne you
    never say, my friends, I didn't warn you. *(She exits.)*

SHAKESPEARE: *(He enters, facing the stage, looks about and slowly turns as he speaks.)* Well, well . . . I greet you now, my dears,
    after a pause of some four hundred years.

ROMEO: How strange, to see our maker in the flesh,
    who fished for us in time and did enmesh
    our hearts and minds in his far-reaching net,
    who taught us what to know and to forget.

SHAKESPEARE: *(Regards his creatures.)* My gentles, let me look at you
    a moment.

OTHELLO: My Lord.

SHAKESPEARE: Oh, not really. How marvelous to see you.
    Hello Hamlet, or I do forget myself.

HAMLET: Master!

SHAKESPEARE: . . . and Romeo . . . so.
    I have aged and you have not. You're
    much the same as I remember you.

ROMEO: Then share with us your aged wisdom, Master.

SHAKESPEARE: *(He chuckles.)* Ah, Romeo, not so fast.
    When young we do learn something from the old.
    But, as we age, our teachers become younger,
    till lastly all our wisdom and experience
    sits at the feet of youth and innocence.

OTHELLO: Dear Master, we are here to speak of love,
    the wonderous subject all must wonder of.
    What we know of it we have learned from you
    so tell us, please, from whence your truths you drew.

SHAKESPEARE: *(He thinks this over.)* Though I made thee, I've not
    the slightest trace
    of what made me, my friends. We could say God.
    But if we praise him for my gifts and grace
    who blame we for respects in which I'm odd?
    Sometimes love's golden beauty was my curse

and yet the inspiration for my verse.
Here's good and evil intertwined again.
From whence the deep, dark pow'rs that move us men?

HAMLET: Questions? Questions? What royal jest is this,
that you the font to whom we turn for truth,
doth echo back upon our puzzled ears
the ignorance we'd hoped to have dispelled.

SHAKESPEARE: Patience, good Prince. Even our Savior
taught in parables. And even Socrates
showed that by plowing up assumptions,
uprooting the rich growth of prejudice,
he could lead minds to those sweet realms of thought
they'd not have reached by way of drowsy sermons.

ROMEO: Teach as you will, dear Will, but having made us—

SHAKESPEARE: To say I *made* thee, Romeo, stretches truth.
I *found* thee, in a common tale of love.
But what I did was give thee life and breath.
Where theretofore your blood was printer's ink
I gave you tongue and turned your blood to fire.

ROMEO: That's close enough, dear Master, to creation.
For even God, our Father, makes our bones
and flesh of prior living matter.

HAMLET: But understand the substance of our plea.
We have the bitter fate in common
of having died for love, when surely all
would have preferred to live for it.

SHAKESPEARE: For it. For it? For what, Hamlet?

HAMLET: Questions again! For love!

SHAKESPEARE: Love. The word is loosely used.
It's not the thing itself but merely symbol,
a coin which of itself is nothing
yet stands for treasure b'yond Cleopatra's dreams.
We love this, love that, love everything and nothing.
Love sea, love air, love trifles, baubles, toys.

OTHELLO: Some men love pain.

ROMEO: Some gamblers love to lose.

HAMLET: Some men, gone vilely mad, love excrement. *(Romeo reacts
with distaste.)*

OTHELLO: Some fornicate with beasts or with the dead!

SHAKESPEARE: And there is love of country.

OTHELLO: Indeed. Your heart so warmed to England, did it not?

SHAKESPEARE: This royal throne of kings, this scepter'd isle,
 this earth of majesty, this seat of Mars,
 this other Eden, demi-paradise;
 this fortress built by Nature for herself
 against infection and the hand of war;
 this happy breed of men, this little world;
 this precious stone set in the silver sea,
 which serves it in the office of a wall,
 or as a moat defensive to a house,
 against the envy of less happier lands;
 this blessed plot, this earth, this realm, this England,
 this nurse, this teeming womb of royal kings,
 fear'd by their breed and famous by their birth,
 renowned for their deeds as far from home—
 for Christian service and true chivalry—
 as is the sepulchre in stubborn Jewry
 of the world's ransom, blessed Mary's Son:
 this land of such dear souls, this dear, dear land,
 dear for her reputation through the world,
 is now leas'd out—I die pronouncing it—
 like to a tenement, or pelting farm:
 England, bound in with the triumphant sea,
 whose rocky shore beats back the envious siege
 of watery Neptune, is now bound in with shame,
 with inky blots, and rotten parchment bonds:
 That England, that was wont to conquer others,
 hath made a shameful conquest of itself.
 Ah! would the scandal vanish with my life,
 how happy then were my ensuing death.

 So love, dear friends, like all our other treasures,
 is what it does. For all its beauty
 it can and does o'erpow'r our sickly wills,
 makes us as helpless as this ancient trunk
 (He indicates an armless, legless Roman statue.)
 sans arms, sans legs, sans even loving member,
 that would, were it not also without tongue,
 spin us a tale or two. What rude barbarian
 did desecrate a temple, smash this idol!
 He too, no doubt, would prate to us of love.
OTHELLO: Some say, my Lord, there's sex behind all love.

SHAKESPEARE: Behind it? Well, that's as good a place for it as any.
But all? Beware such words as "all," "always,"
"Ever," "never."
All rules have their exceptions.

HAMLET: All rules, my Lord?

SHAKESPEARE: *(He laughs.)* No, love and sex have intimate connection
but in the fact of their connection are established twain.

ROMEO: *(Eagerly)* A thing is not connected to itself but to another
thing.

SHAKESPEARE: *(Sarcastically)* Your grasp of the apparent seems secure.

HAMLET: Good master, might we grace this conversation
with what we're told was your supreme achievement
in the poetry of love? . . . the sonnets?

SHAKESPEARE: Why the sonnets?

HAMLET: Because, dear Master, we have traded dreams of love
but never was a better subject sweeter sung
than in those songs of music, sunlight, wine,
those magic incantations that evoke
the sweetest oaths that lovers ever spoke.

ROMEO: And in the knowing them, my Lord,
there'll be the greater sense of knowing thee.

HAMLET: Pray, Master, do recite them for us now,
each syllable a blossom on a bough,
each line a branch, and ev'ry poem a tree
in whose cool shade the heart rests gratefully.

SHAKESPEARE: A graceful turn of phrase, dear Hamlet.
(He picks up a quill pen and makes a note of it.)
I'll gladly speak of beauty in distress,
for thence, you see, does inspiration come,
and when our hearts would otherwise be dumb
we can take seeds of powerful desire,
commingle them with flame of some past fire,
whence add not what we see but what we need
and thus make manna on which hearts may feed.
But not the sonnets. Not *tonight*. Not *here*.

OTHELLO: But, sir, of love we'd gladly hear you speak.

SHAKESPEARE: And so I shall, my friend of organ voice.
I see the mem'ry of it stirs your blood, as well it should.
Love quickens all the senses.
Other slow arts entirely keep the brain,
and therefore, finding barren practisers,

scarce show a harvest of their heavy toil;
but love, first learned in a lady's eyes,
lives not alone immured in the brain,
but, with the motion of all elements,
courses as swift as thought in every power,
and gives to every power a double power,
above their functions and their offices.
It adds a precious seeing to the eye;
a lover's eyes will gaze an eagle blind;
a lover's ear will hear the lowest sound,
when the suspicious head of theft is stopp'd:
Love's feeling is more soft and sensible
than are the tender horns of cockled snails:
Love's tongue proves dainty Bacchus gross in taste.
For valor, is not Love a Hercules,
still climbing trees in the Hesperides?
Subtle as Sphinx; as sweet and musical
as bright Apollo's lute, strung with his hair;
and when Love speaks, the voice of all the gods
makes heaven drowsy with the harmony.

WOMAN: *(We hear her voice. She is not seen.)* Sweet William.

SHAKESPEARE: Who's that? *(He looks about.)*

WOMAN: You know perfectly well.
Your creatures wish to hear a *sonnet,* Will.
Is it so very much to ask?

SHAKESPEARE: Where *are* you?

WOMAN: In your heart, my dear. As ever.
I'd rather not, but I command you.

SHAKESPEARE: *(He frowns, thinks of resisting, but cannot.)* When in
disgrace with fortune and men's eyes,
I all alone beweep my outcast state,
and trouble deaf heaven with my bootless cries,
and look upon myself, and curse my fate,
wishing me like to one more rich in hope,
featured like him, like him with friends possess'd,
desiring this man's art and that man's scope,
with what I most enjoy contented least;
yet in these thoughts myself almost despising,
hap'ly I think on thee, and then my state,
like to the lark at break of day arising
from sullen earth, sings hymns at heaven's gate;

for thy sweet love remember'd such wealth brings
that then I scorn to change my state with kings.
HAMLET: Bravo! Beautiful.
ROMEO: Ah, had I sung those words to Juliet.
OTHELLO: You'd still not have escaped your fortune's net.
SHAKESPEARE: And then I wrote . . .

When to the sessions of sweet silent thought
I summon up remembrance of things past,
I sigh the lack of many a thing I sought,
and with old woes new wail my dear time's waste:
Then I can drown an eye, unused to flow,
for precious friends hid in death's dateless night,
and weep afresh love's long since cancell'd woe,
and moan the expense of many a vanish'd sight:
then I can grieve at grievances foregone,
and heavily from woe to woe tell o'er
the sad account of fore-bemoaned moan,
which I new pay as if not paid before.
But if the while I think on thee, dear friend,
all losses are restored and sorrows end.

HAMLET: There is, Master, in all those words a sense
    that one might not pay Time's dread recompense.
SHAKESPEARE: Ah, no, dear Hamlet. Time in time will win
    for we must die, in virtue or in sin.
ROMEO: And yet Love feels the need that it must fling
    a challenge to resist Death's painful sting.
OTHELLO: *(Furiously)* Ah, death, that rudely puts a stop to love,
    that lays a monster's hand on silken throats.
    I would it were a man so I could *kill* it!
SHAKESPEARE: *(He shakes his head sadly.)* And in the doing in its fate
    fulfill it.
    No, no, dear friends, dear loves of now and then,
    there's quite enough of beauty for most men.
    though we go to the country of the blind
    we are recalled by those we leave behind.
ROMEO: Dear Master, speak no more to us of death
    but of that living Spring of Love's first breath.
SHAKESPEARE: Shall I compare thee to a summer's day?
    Thou art more lovely and more temperate.

Rough winds do shake the darling buds of May,
and summer's lease hath all too short a date:
Sometime too hot the eye of heaven shines,
and often is his gold complexion dimm'd;
and every fair from fair sometimes declines,
by chance or nature's changing course untrimm'd;
but thy eternal summer shall not fade,
nor lose possession of that fair thou owest;
nor shall Death brag thou wander'st in his shade,
when in eternal lines to time thou grow'st:
So long as men can breathe, or eyes can see,
so long lives this, and this gives life to thee.

Young friend, of tender years, surely you know
that love is partly riches, partly woe.
Salt tears are what do make its laughter sweet;
lovers must part if once again they'd meet.
And so I said once to my dearest heart
these words that sought to unite Truth with Art.
Then hate me when thou wilt; if ever, now;
now, while the world is bent my deeds to cross,
join with the spite of fortune. Make me bow,
and do *not* drop in for an after-loss:
Ah, do not, when my heart hath 'scaped this sorrow,
come in the rearward of a conquer'd woe;
give not a windy night a rainly morrow,
to linger out a purposed overthrow.

If thou wilt leave me, do not leave me last.
when other petty griefs have done their spite,
but in the onset come: Then so shall I taste
at first the very worst of fortune's might;
and other strains of woe, which now seem woe,
compared with loss of thee will not seem so.
ROMEO: Ah, woe. The sad impediment of fate
    that robbed my Juliet of her rightful state.
SHAKESPEARE: Oh, let me not to the marriage of true minds
    Admit impediments. Love is not love
    which alters when it alteration finds,
    or bends with the remover to remove:
    O, no! It is an ever-fixed mark,

that looks on tempests and is never shaken;
it is the star to every wandering bark,
whose worth's unknown, although his height be taken.
Love's not Time's fool, though rosy lips and cheeks
within his bending sickle's compass come;
Love alters not with his brief hours and weeks,
but bears it out even to the edge of doom.
If this be error and upon me proved,
I never wrote, nor no man ever loved. *(Woman appears to one
side, in shadow.)*

HAMLET: How sad, dear Master, we did never meet
the lady who received your garlands sweet,
who knew your poetry and your embrace.
What we would give to gaze upon that face.

WOMAN: *(Derisively)* Tell them, Will.

SHAKESPEARE: —what?

WOMAN: Reveal the inspiration for your singing sonnets.

SHAKESPEARE: Oh, yes.
Why, you, my dear, did so inflame my soul—

WOMAN: Oh, stop!
Should truth be partial when it could be whole?

SHAKESPEARE: I hope you realize what you are doing?

WOMAN: The truth shall make you free, my Lord.

SHAKESPEARE: Irreverent bitch!

WOMAN: Not so, my love. I do revere your art.
Reveal the dream of which it was a part.

SHAKESPEARE: *(To himself)* Dream?

WOMAN: Nightmare, rather?

HAMLET: Stop badgering this man! Master, pray tell
Who was the woman that you sang so well?

SHAKESPEARE: She stands before you.

WOMAN: Confession, Will! It's so good for the soul.

OTHELLO: Was there another woman too?

WOMAN: What's this? Woman, you say? Ah, yes. I see.
You have such knowledge as was giv'n to thee
so not enough to know of his own story,
to tell of which was guilt and which was glory.

OTHELLO: Guilt? No, Master, prithee, say not so.
You are our god, as such dispensing woe
to those of us whose follies did deserve it.
My mind is ill at ease. Do not unnerve it.

ROMEO: Pray, clarify the question you did ask
    when Hamlet's inquiry took you to task.
HAMLET: Yes. You seemed surprised.
    Is there some mystery we've not surmised?
WOMAN: I would say so.
SHAKESPEARE: But most of all to me
    who did not make himself, though I made thee.
WOMAN: But since they've asked you owe them, Will, forsooth,
    what, if it be not beauty, is the truth.
SHAKESPEARE: These sonnets were not written to be sent
    save to the ones to whom they were dispatched.
    To publish them was never my intent.
    I never planned that those eggs should be hatched.
    Some of the sonnets were by her inspired
    by whom my heart was kindled, blown, and fired.
    But most, my friends, by whom I was enthralled.
    Henry Wriothesly, Earl of Southampton called.
ROMEO: What!?
HAMLET: God's wounds!
WOMAN: Ha! *(Exits upstairs laughing.)*
OTHELLO: Say no, my Lord. Deny this staggering story!
    Our God a lover of his selfsame kind?
    What jest is this? I pray, affirm your glory.
    Refute the lie yours was a woman's mind.
SHAKESPEARE: Peace, brave Othello. You shall know the truth
    and by it, said our Savior, yet be freed.
    Truth is *not* always beauty, but uncouth
    and raw, regardless of our need.
    Your Desdemona was a loyal wife
    and yet you drew away her breath of life.
    Your kind decides on murder, know it well.
    I never willed to make my private hell.
    What crueler fate than that which paints the smile
    of sweetest love on that which men call vile.
    Your tortures were as nothing to my own;
    for you were dreams, but I was flesh and bone.

    The man who loves a woman can prepare
    a warm security no fire can burn.
    They can grow old together, raise an heir,
    spend passion's gold, and see its rich return.

Their love is open and a guide to all;
but those who are beguiled by their own kind
know not where that security to find.
Their love compulsion, their achievement shame,
and, worst of all, they know not whom to blame.

OTHELLO: Blame?

SHAKESPEARE: We do not build our separate souls, my friends.
Those who are fully given to one or other
at least can soon foretell their fate.
But others tremble on a fearful balance.
But stay Othello. There was more to me
than what the lidded eyes of gossip see,
for I was married when a bumpkin boy
to my dear Anne, who brought me simple joy.
I'd been a heady youth, in some ways wild.
We married after Anne was got with child.
The Hathaways and Shakespeares equal were,
in station modest, reputation fair.
The child we named Susanah. Later twins,
and thus my placid married life begins.

ROMEO: What, married? Then the same as any man.

SHAKESPEARE: So once I thought myself. But in the span
of ten short years my certainty was shaken.
Southampton spoke. My mind was overtaken.

HAMLET: Inconstant man. Well, then, were you at least
faithful to him whose fame your art increased?

SHAKESPEARE: Both yes and no. I wrote a million words
that flocked around his head, adoring birds,
singing his praises, grateful for his crumbs.
But to what Paradise temptation comes
as seemingly it must in ev'ry case.
I met that strange Dark Lady whose fair face
enchanted me, controlled me, whose warm smile
enticed my poor inconstant heart the while.

WOMAN: *(Dressed now in black, she sneers at Othello, Romeo, and Hamlet.)* You fools. To think your world has come to this.
Your god has feet of clay. He was remiss
in every effort to achieve one love.
His failure was the stuff you're builded of.

ROMEO: Oh, this is more than my young heart can bear,
that one's Creator's not omnipotent!

He *wrote* of perfect love but found it ne'er.

I never knew what my own statements meant.

OTHELLO: It is a rude and staggering surprise.

I am confused. Every foundation shakes.

We were not made of that in which he's wise,

but of the shattered shards of his mistakes.

HAMLET: Unfaithful to his dear Anne with his fair Earl,

then traitrous to Southampton with a girl,

or woman rather, that Dark Lady who

for so long hid her features from our view.

Unable to find joy or peace with him,

enslaved by her, his vision growing dim,

forced to acknowledge his fierce debt to lust,

doing not what he should but what he must.

Could you not be what you had willed to be?

SHAKESPEARE: *(Sadly)* Ah, Hamlet. To be or not to be—

HAMLET: That *is* the question!

SHAKESPEARE: Think not that I had not considered

seeking death before it came for me?

HAMLET: Do not we all, if truth were known?

Whether 'tis nobler in the mind to suffer

the slings and arrows of outrageous fortune,

or to take arms against a sea of troubles—

SHAKESPEARE: There are some troubles arms are weak against.

HAMLET: To die—

SHAKESPEARE: To sleep. No more. And, by a sleep to say we end

The heartache and the thousand natural shocks

That flesh is heir to. 'Tis a consummation devoutly to be wished.

HAMLET: To *die.*

SHAKESPEARE: To sleep. To sleep, perchance to dream.

SHAKESPEARE AND HAMLET: Aye there's the rub.

For who would bear the whips and scorns of time,

the oppressor's wrong, the proud man's contumely,

HAMLET: the pangs of despised love?

SHAKESPEARE: Ah, who would grunt and sweat under a weary life

but that the dread of something after death—

HAMLET: the undiscovered country from whose bourn

no traveller returns, puzzles the will,

and makes us rather bear those ills we have

than fly to others that we know not of?

ROMEO: But you did nothing of the kind, I trust.

SHAKESPEARE: Your trust's secure, for I had such a thirst for life
    I'd not overturn it's cup.

WOMAN: But still, with none of these,
    Southampton, mistress, Anne,
    successful as a lover or a man.

HAMLET: And yet a genius! If truly all the world's a stage
    this was the strangest casting in any age.

OTHELLO: What mystery genius, the magic flower
    that grows without warm sun, rich soil, or shower,
    that flashes like a meteor by night
    from darkness come, to realms beyond our sight.

HAMLET: It is not any other god's reward.
    Where virtue need not dwell its wings have soared.

ROMEO: In this we creatures are like mortal men
    who know not whence they came, nor why, nor when.

SHAKESPEARE: *(To audience)* Our God once suffered quite alone and so,
    created mortal men to suffer woe.
    Foreseeing tears, created men to weep them,
    for suicides, made cliffs that they might leap them,
    foreseeing pain, made men to shriek by night.
    Content not with his heaven, made a hell,
    contented not with faith, made doubt as well.

HAMLET: So man is now a mass of contradictions.
    Forgive this day our daily maledictions.

ROMEO: But how can this, our Master, have loved Anne
    but later seen in Southampton, a man,
    the answer to some secret need long hid?
    I must know *why* rather than *what* he did.

HAMLET: You shall not know, dear Romeo. The mind
    will ne'er completely its extent unwind.
    There's more to all of us than we shall know;
    we're injured quick but do recover slow.

    What a piece of work is man.
    How noble in reason! How infinite in faculty!
    In form and moving how express and admirable!
    In action how like an angel! In apprehension
    how like a god! The beauty of the world!
    The paragon of animals! And yet, to me,
    what is this quintessence of dust?

Man delights not me;
no, nor woman neither, though by your smiling
you seem to say so.

ROMEO: Master, was Southampton, —er, —your—

SHAKESPEARE: My only fall from grace?

ROMEO: Yes.

SHAKESPEARE: He was. And thus the mystery more.

WOMAN: Wait, gentlemen; there's some injustice here,
some lack of proper balance in the scales.
I, Woman, know what this man held dear;
mine was the strongest breeze that filled his sails.
Southampton was his patron.
(To Shakespeare) Tell them now
how slavishly to power you would bow.
Beguiled by palace, by gold, by silk,
ambition fawned on nobles and their ilk.

SHAKESPEARE: Once more into the breach, dear friends.

WOMAN: He was your patron and your earthly Lord.
In part it was his station you adored.
But it was never seemly to my taste
two such attractive men should go to waste.
Directly to the one, then to the other,
I proved a sister better than a—
(She approaches Shakespeare seductively.)
Tell them, Will, how madly you succumbed,
how deep desire its siren solo strummed.
You were my slave; you lived from kiss to kiss.
Your fevers these cool fingers once could soothe.
Your arms could nothing better do than this;
you loved me, Will. I drove you mad with lust.
Tell the truth, 'ere you return to dust.
For there was more than lust, Will.
Love, sweet love! 'Twas Paradise
within these arms and looking in these eyes.
You sang those eyes, you bastard!
Confess! Recall? My mistress eyes are nothing like the sun.
Coral is far more than her lips red;

SHAKESPEARE: if snow be white, why then her breasts are dun;
if hairs be wires, black wires grow on her head.
I have seen roses damask'd, red, and white,
but no such roses see I in her cheeks;

and in some perfumes is there more delight
than in the breath that from my mistress reeks.
I love to hear her speak, yet well I know
that music hath a far more pleasing sound:
I grant I never saw a goddess go.
My mistress, when she walks, treads on the ground.
But by heaven, I think my love as rare,
as any she belied with false compare.

WOMAN: The feeling's coming back, I see.
You loved me, Will, and I had need of thee.

OTHELLO: Well said, Dark Lady.

SHAKESPEARE: In the old age black was not counted fair.

OTHELLO: How's that?

SHAKESPEARE: A wightly wanton with a velvet brow,
with two pitch-balls stuck in her face for eyes;
ay, and, by heaven, one that will do the deed
though Argus were her eunuch and her guard:
And I to sigh for her! to watch for her!
to pray for her! Go to; it is a plague
that Cupid will impose for my neglect
of his almighty dreadful little might.

WOMAN: Come, Will, be manly. Take me in your arms.
Don't tell me you'll be cool to such warm charms.
You loved me with your hands; tell us no lies;
you loved me with your mouth, and with your eyes.

OTHELLO: Good woman, must you taunt this haunted man?
You've made your point. He loves you as he can.
You took him from Southampton. We applaud.
He loves you, whether you were saint or bawd.

WOMAN: What do you judge, if we would judgment do?
I made your Master slave; Southampton, too.

HAMLET: What? You say *both* men were in your power?
Good Master, pray, is this her truthful hour?

WOMAN: *(She laughs.)* You were no expert, Will, on Love. You know
it.
And if you doubt, why, all your life doth show it.

SHAKESPEARE: *(He nods, sadly.)* Hamlet, my dear, came near the heart
of truth
in saying we may educate ourselves on ev'ry
matter save the weightiest of all.
Why, if 'twere otherwise philosophers would be

the greatest lovers. But this is clearly not the case.
And even Saints, whose gift is loving God,
are seen to turn their backs on mothers, wives.
Nor poets, scholars, artisans of music
are better at the art than simple men.
There are no Michelangelos of love.
Observe, dear visitors, without whose ears
I have not any voice, that here before you
stand four failures who—

WOMAN: Five.

SHAKESPEARE: I stand corrected. Five failures, at a game
the which, if anthropologists are right,
we've had a million years of practice at.
So whether love is made or found or felt,
treat it, I pray you, as a precious gem
but far more dear than golden ornaments.

OTHELLO: You pray in saintly verse, dear Master.
Foolhardy were we to oppose your course.

SHAKESPEARE: Saintly? No, sir, never saintly I.
Our Savior, Christ, forsooth, uniquely taught,
where any man might bid us love our friends
that we should love our sharpest enemies.

OTHELLO: That this is wisdom of a pure, astounding beauty
I'd be last to deny. But when we search
for instances, examples, writs of proof,
ah, there, 'twould seem, we enter realms so barren,
were we to march abroad till we had found
one single instance of a kiss bestowed
on hated brow, one moment of sweet love
for him who robs, or does us any harm,
we'd march, I fear, to our unholy graves.

WOMAN: Creation! Creativity! Is it the harmony
of intellect with wild emotion
or the raging conflict of the two?
What say you now, sweet William?

SHAKESPEARE: The ancient argument for freedom of the will
buttressed by Aquinas, learned doctor,
is weakest where it touches the emotions.
A man decides to move this way or that,
to sit, to stand, to speak, to spend, to save.
Emotions, on the other hand, are in response

to what takes place about us. If a spear
prods at our ribs we lightning-quick do fear
or shout our anger. One enchanting smile
can in the instant strike into the heart
with devastation equal to the sword's.

WOMAN: I see, Will, you're still stumbling in the dark.

SHAKESPEARE: What?

WOMAN: Your rambling proves you're unequal to my question.
You can't explain your creativity
any more than you know why you longed for me.
You men make haste—you know it—not to wed us;
the object of your will is more to bed us.
And if we'll not have that, you'll swear, of course,
to have by marriage what's not yours by force.

SHAKESPEARE: Have you no mem'ry of me on my knees?

WOMAN: I have. And while you spoke of faith and trust
you worshipped at the altar of your lust.

HAMLET: What's wrong with that? It's nature's instrument!

WOMAN: 'Tis true, and sometimes strong, and sometimes bent.
It's not your manhood I attack. Hypocrisy!
Your pompous souls can blow both cold and hot.
But even when you breathe the words "I love you"
you're speaking of yourselves now, are you not?

SHAKESPEARE: Dear lady, peace. Could we at least decide
there's beauty in the hope of each young bride?
I speak now, understand, of pure ideal.
Surely there is something you must feel
would be most seemly if it could exist.
Some dream that springs when lovers first have kissed.
Concede, if—if again I say—
into your life could walk this very day
some gentle man and yet protector strong,
true, brave, yet lover of a song,
father and philosopher as well.
If you'd be shrew to him the world would scorn
for 'tis from such men hope for all is born.
But picture him tall at thy bedside now.
Fie! Fie! Unknit that threatening unkind brow:
And dart not scornful glances from those eyes,
to wound thy lord, thy king, thy governor:
It bolts thy beauty as frosts do bite the meads,

confounds thy fame as whirlwinds shake fair buds,
and in no sense is mete or amiable.
A woman moved is like a fountain troubled,
muddy, ill-seeming, thick, bereft of beauty;
and while it is so, none so dry or thirsty
will deign to sip or touch one drop of it.

WOMAN: *(She begins to weaken. She speaks with utter sincerity,
simplicity.)* My husband could be Lord, my life, my keeper?
My head, my sovereign; one that cares for me
and for my maintenance commits his body
to painful labor both by sea and land?

ROMEO: *Yes!* To watch the night in storms, the day in cold
whilst thou liest warm at home, secure and safe;
and craves no other tribute at thy hands
but love, fair looks, and true obedience;
too little payment for so great a debt.

OTHELLO: Such duty as the subject owes the Prince
even such a woman oweth such a man.

WOMAN: You speak as to an unbelieving heart,
a Thomas doubting, hating yet his doubt.
There's no denying peace is prized o'er war.
I'm bitter from experience, true, but yes
there's that in me that freely will confess
I cherish still the sweetness of the dream
that in my girlhood shimmering true did seem.
I love what should be, as I fear what is.
But truly something in me wants to say:
I am ashamed that women are so simple
to offer war where they should kneel for peace;
or seek for rule, supremacy, and sway,
when they are bound to serve, love, and obey.
Why are our bodies soft and weak and smooth,
unapt to toil and trouble in the world,
but that our soft conditions and our hearts
should well agree with our external parts?
Come, come, you froward and unable worms!
My mind hath been as big as one of yours,
my heart as great, my reason hap'ly more,
to bandy word for word and frown for frown;
but now I see our lances are but straws,
our strength is weak, our weakness past compare,

that seeming to be most which we indeed least are,
then find a heart in which your trust to put
and place your hands below your husband's foot:
In token of which duty, if he please,
my hand is ready, may it do him ease.
(She and Will Shakespeare clasp hands.)

SHAKESPEARE: My lady! *(He kneels, kissing her hand. Their hands wrestle briefly for the upper position.)*

What's this? Rebellion?
So briefly saint,
and then again a hellion?

WOMAN: *(She laughs, but warmly.)* Ah, no, my Lord.
Your mate I'd hap'ly be.
but only under full equality.

ROMEO: Well, why not? Love is truth
and truth makes free.

WOMAN: And slave to slave forever we may be.

SHAKESPEARE: *(He thinks, briefly.)* Agreed, my love.

WOMAN: My world and all are thine.

SHAKESPEARE: My life is yours. And all that's yours is mine.

HAMLET: And so away to bed, good friends, we go.
How wisely you're instructed by our show
depends on you, not on what we did teach.
So, honor the observance or the breach.

OTHELLO: Each man's his own instructor, after all.
It has been thus, yes, ever since the time
when Eve, 'tis said, did tempt her lover lone
who blamed her, since of parents he had none.

ROMEO: All's well that ends well, not to coin a phrase.
Now go we on our predetermined ways.

SHAKESPEARE: Thus—as you like it—lady, and dear friends,
Our much ado of nothing gently ends.

STEVE: *(He enters, addresses others, then audience.)*
Our revels now are ended. These our actors,
as we've suggested, were all spirits and
are melted into air, into thin air;
and, like the baseless fabric of such visions,
the cloud-capped towers, the gorgeous palaces,
the solemn temples, the great globe itself,
yea, all which it inherit, shall dissolve,
and, like this insubstantial pageant faded,

leave not a rack behind. We are such stuff
as dreams are made on, and our little life
is rounded with a sleep.
Between the first awaking and the final drowse
those are the richest who are loved and love.
And if we would increase the moral monsters in our midst
'tis very simple. We need but deprive
young souls of that great heat and light
without which even God's designs are ineffectual.
Good night.